'Professor Aguilar's book moves across continents and religious traditions with the ease and grace that comes from the depth and empathy of a lifetime's familiarity and study. Whether meeting Buddhists in Chile, Sikhs in India or Hindus in Scotland, we feel the personal friendships and experiences which have inspired him. However, its particular strength and uniqueness is the way he explores the places of the hermit's life as a site of meaning and sacred connectedness. Both those fresh to interreligious dialogue and lifelong practitioners and scholars in the discipline will find fresh insights and perspectives in the pages of this work.'

– *Paul Hedges, Associate Professor of Interreligious Studies at RSIS, NTU, Singapore and author of* Towards Better Disagreement: Religion and Atheism in Dialogue

'Dialogue in silence; speaking without words; this complex book explores the possibility of connection between faiths in the sacred space that silence allows and is a useful addition to the growing literature on interfaith dialogue.'

– *Dr Maureen Sier, Director of Interfaith Scotland*

'In a world awash with chatter and superficial talk-fests, the choice of solitude and silence is spiritually challenging. Memory lives in silence. God is found there. With a deep and movingly autobiographical thread, *The Way of the Hermit* creatively probes the contribution of the eremitic life to Christian interfaith encounter.'

– *Professor Douglas Pratt, University of Waikato & University of Bern*

'Digging deep and drawing generously from the wells of experience and expertise, Professor Aguilar throws open the richness of dialogue that happens in the depths of silence and solitude that characterize a life of hermitage. Theologically imaginative and spiritually inspiring, the book recovers the potential of presence, poetry and prayer for dialogue in fresh and fascinating ways.'

– *The Reverend Dr Peniel Jesudason Rufus Rajkumar,*
Programme Executive, Interreligious Dialogue and
Cooperation, World Council of Churches, Switzerland

by the same author

Christian Ashrams, Hindu Caves and Sacred Rivers
Christian-Hindu Monastic Dialogue in India 1950–1993
Mario I. Aguilar
ISBN 978 1 78592 086 8
eISBN 978 1 78450 347 5
Studies in Religion and Theology series

of related interest

Towards Better Disagreement
Religion and Atheism in Dialogue
Paul Hedges
ISBN 978 1 78592 057 8
eISBN 978 1 78450 316 1

Re-enchanting the Activist
Spirituality and Social Change
Keith Hebden
ISBN 978 1 78592 041 7
eISBN 978 1 78450 295 9

Sadness, Depression and the Dark Night of the Soul
Glòria Durà-Vilà
Foreword by Professor Roland Littlewood
ISBN 978 1 78592 056 1
eISBN 978 1 78450 313 0

THE
WAY
OF
THE
HERMIT

Interfaith Encounters in
Silence and Prayer

Mario I. Aguilar

Jessica Kingsley *Publishers*
London and Philadelphia

First published in 2017
by Jessica Kingsley Publishers
73 Collier Street
London N1 9BE, UK
and
400 Market Street, Suite 400
Philadelphia, PA 19106, USA

www.jkp.com

Library of Congress Cataloging in Publication Data
Title: The way of the hermit : interfaith encounters in silence and prayer / Mario I.
Aguilar.
Description: Philadelphia : Jessica Kingsley Publishers, 2017.
Identifiers: LCCN 2016051852 | ISBN 9781785920899 (alk. paper)
Subjects: LCSH: Hermits. | Prayer. | Contemplation. | Silence--Religious
    aspects. | Christianity and other religions--Hinduism. |
    Hinduism--Relations--Christianity.
Classification: LCC BX2845 .A38 2017 | DDC 261.2/45--dc23 LC record available
at https://lccn.loc.gov/2016051852

British Library Cataloguing in Publication Data
A CIP catalogue record for this book is available from the British Library

ISBN 978 1 78592 089 9
eISBN 978 1 78450 354 3

Printed and bound in the United States

Dedicated to the memory of
Roberto Tello Verdejo (+2016)

To his daughter, Glenda Tello

To Sara Ann Catherine

CONTENTS

Acknowledgements

I wanted to be a hermit, even when nobody understood why, attracted by the sand and the memories of the Desert Fathers, the Hindu *sadhus* and the Muslim Bedouins. My first encounter with sand, camels and sky was when I lived in Garba Tulla, northern Kenya, among pastoralist Boorana, and where for a couple of years I sat in front of my house looking at the stars and knowing that finally God was present in that firmament and in that blue night of the desert.[1] In my younger years, I had sat on the veranda of Roberto Tello's home in Chile talking to Glenda Tello about the sand and the presence of God as written and portrayed by Carlo Carretto in his letters from the desert, a man who followed the steps of Charles de Foucauld.[2] For in my life I never wanted to have a mediated description of God, I wanted to meet God face to face, just the two of us to talk and talk. I discovered that for many years I enjoyed sitting on that sand with a God who came many times and in silence sat beside me, while Mohamed, the watchman in Garba Tulla, prayed his Muslim rosary and stood armed to make sure that I was safe. God transformed me, moulded me, so that slowly and over the years my words disappeared and his silence embraced me. When I left the sand, I had lost interest in preaching and speaking, and I only wanted to sit beside God. However, the God of Mohamed the watchman had shown me that he was the same person and the dry hand of a nomad, a shepherd and a warrior took mine and made it into a different hand.

I felt the same silence and closeness when I visited Luxor and the Valley of the Kings in Egypt and sat for a long time on that sand of God, of pharaohs and of the Israelites. As the archaeologist Howard Carter knew, there was something hidden in the sand. I knew that the God of the sand was hidden in silence but very much present in the lives of those digging and hoping to unearth wealth and happiness. I unearthed silence, and the silence made me happy. God was sitting with me again on the sand and he was silent, how wonderfully close and how wonderfully silent. It was the same feeling that I felt when I arrived in India and the heat and the dust. Those holy men and women also made that miracle happen: God was sitting beside me once again in silence with that powerful silence of chaos and life that embraced my senses and my soul, with Buddhists in Dharamsala, with Hindus in Delhi and Amritsar, and with Sikhs of the Golden Temple under the heat of the day and the silence of God. I remained silent with young Buddhist Pema at the top of the Himalayan hills, and I felt that the God who had been sitting with me for years came again and sat beside us while the peaks of the Himalaya moved in their silence and spoke loudly through the rain, the clouds and the mist.

This work has been in the making for years because for years I have been more and more silent, and God has emptied my words and has taken them away so that the two of us could have a long sitting together that over the years has extended to Buddhists and Hindus. It is in the silence of Arunachala Hermitage that I salute the many masters that have guided me in silence and who while showing me their wisdom have left me in the complete freedom to be with God, the two of us, in a silent cosmic symphony, in the great Amen and the great OM that unites all humanity in one word and in silence. This is an autobiographical work and a theological reflection on the possibilities of a Christian in dialogue with Hindus without words, without matter, without objective, without borders. Because God has been sitting at these dialogues in silence I can only say that I have felt very close to Buddhists and Hindus as well as Jews and Muslims, and that, in those moments in the sand and in the silence, I have been a Christian, and a Hindu, and a Buddhist, and a Jew, and a Muslim, because I am no more than a human being sitting at the feet of God. I am not the important player but the God who comes every day and every minute in such silence.

I acknowledge the love and generosity of Glenda Tello, and I honour the memory of her father who in times of search and healing gave me entry to his orderly and well-provided-for world. I acknowledge the wisdom and teachings of Geshe Lakhdor in Dharamsala, of Ramesh Babu and family in Amritsar, and of Professor Balwant Singh Dhillon and staff at Guru Nanak Dev University.

In Amritsar, I acknowledge the kind and supportive silence of Singh Sahib Giani Joginder Singh, Jathedar of Sri Akal Takht Sahib (2000–2008), and of the silent *sadhus* of Arunachala who didn't smile at my foolishness but shared their silence. My gratitude to Dr Gordon T. Barclay, companion in dreams and adventures, and to Dr Eric Stoddart and Dr John Perry as associate directors of the CSRP of the School of Divinity, University of St Andrews.

I acknowledge particularly the generosity of Kabir Babu, with whom I have had long and sustained conversations about Christianity and Hinduism. My thanks to the Revd Dr Dan Connor for ongoing comments on my work at the seminars and via email and to my former teacher Dr Hans Wijngaards for providing me with a copy of the text for the celebration of the Indian Eucharist. Some chapters of this work were discussed at the weekly seminar of the CSRP of the School of Divinity of the University of St Andrews, and I am grateful to Dr Eve Parker, Mohammed Al-Hinai, Walter Lopes Da Silva, Jake Cowland, Andrew Marin, Alex Lawson, Webster Kameme, James Morris and Kasia Bylow-Antkowiak for comments on different aspects of this work. I acknowledge the ongoing support and friendship of Professor Hugh McDougall, Professor Pascale Fournier, Porsiana Beatrice and Dr Milja Radovic.

Recognizing the close connection between Hinduism and Buddhism I would like to acknowledge conversations in Dharamsala regarding this work with the Tibetan Sikiong Dr Lobsang Sangay, and in London with Kelsang Gyaltsen (Special Representative of His Holiness the Dalai Lama to Europe), Chonpel Tsering (Representative of His Holiness the Dalai Lama to the United Kingdom), Dr Tsering Topgyal (University of Birmingham) and Dr Dibyesh Anand (University of Westminster).

Finally, my thanks to Dr Natalie K. Watson, Senior Commissioning Editor at Jessica Kingsley Publishers, for encouraging me to complete another work under her kind editorship.

Within this work, I have used unpublished poems by Sunra Babu, Ramesh Babu and Kabir Babu. They have expressly given their consent for the reproduction of these poems and I am thankful for their correspondence, explanations and commitment to a journey of dialogue together.

Mario I. Aguilar
Arunachala Hermitage, 31 October 2016
500 years after the Reformation and on the day of the signing
of the agreement of cooperation between Caritas Internationalis
and the Lutheran World Federation World Service

INTRODUCTION

Experiencing Contemplation and Interfaith Dialogue

The way of a hermit is the way of a Christian who has sought his journey with God through the centrality of space contained in a single monastic cell in which his or her life connects with the passing of time. The cell as the locality of the spiritual journey is located outside a monastery, on a hill, inside a cave, beside a beach, or even within an apartment in an urban centre. Time becomes the reality in which God and the hermit meet and in which the hermit and others meet. Minutes, hours, days and years of such eremitic life relate to one individual's search for God and for an ongoing conversation with God in solitude and a daily encounter with other human beings, sentient beings and the whole of creation. However, hermits, because of their way of life seeking holiness and enlightenment, have always attracted other pilgrims who have come closer to a hermitage to seek prayers, encouragement and spiritual affirmation. Thus, in the case of Charles de Foucauld, Abhishiktananda, Thomas Merton and even Mahatma Gandhi, the solitude sought and the renunciation practised led eventually to encounters with others, not only through the challenging of a world around them but in a deep conversation and encounter with practitioners of other faiths and other philosophical systems. Such solitude has been marked by what I have called in my previous work on Christian–Hindu dialogue 'dialogues in history', whereby dialogue is an experience between human beings that starts with friendship and develops into a pilgrimage together.[1] Thus, in *Christian Ashrams, Hindu Caves and Sacred Rivers* I have argued that 'history not only becomes the tool to understand changes in the context of dialogue, but also it becomes the *locus theologicus* where any reflections about religious and divine narratives take place'.[2] Therefore, in this work I explore that eremitic characteristic: a solitude and search for spiritual and self-development that brings unto it the encounter with others and the search for others' experiences of the Absolute.

In contemporary times, hermits have also been part of a monastery or a religious community, and within such communal experience they have chosen to spend time alone near their monastery. Thus, that monastic experience of solitude, such as that experienced by Thomas Merton in his house/hermitage at the Abbey of Gethsemani in Kentucky, has still been located within the principle of stability and monastic obedience (and therefore of authority) of the *cenobium*.[3] It is a fact that monastic cenobitic communities such as the Benedictines and the Cistercians have centred their contemplative life in a cenobium, a community of monks who share a common purpose, a common rule and a communal liturgical life, with a vow of stability and attachment to a particular community, abbey or monastery. Arising out of those monastic communities, and since the beginnings of the Church, there have been Christians that have sought God through personal solitude, with the example of the Fathers of the Desert as the most influential within the history of the Christian Church. However, the most well-known Christian hermits of the twentieth century were those who slowly moved from personal solitude attached to a community to personal solitude and attachment to others outside their initial experience of the cenobium. Those who lived such experience include Charles de Foucauld (North Africa), Henri Le Saux (India) and Thomas Merton (United States), who also shared their deep search for an experiential encounter with other religious and philosophical traditions.

Hermits have made the cell a place where they sit and wait for God to experience the love of God and where they confront the inner challenge of a pilgrimage in solitude through self-discovery. They fight their own demons to free themselves of the aspects of material life that make their listening to God more difficult, and in doing so they become even more aware of those around them. Thus the beginning of the Brief Rule of St Romuald, founder of the Camaldolese Benedictines, exhorts the hermit with the following words: 'Sit in your cell' and 'Put the whole world behind you and forget it.'[4] These instructions provide a continuity to the early Desert Fathers who interpreted Jesus' time in the desert as a formative one related to their knowledge of God. Abba Moses, for example, provided the following instruction: 'Go, sit in your cell, and your cell will teach you everything.'[5]

EREMITIC LIFE AND INTERFAITH DIALOGUE

This sitting in one's cell becomes the first place where the hermit converses with the God of many peoples and many faiths and learns to leave attachments and prejudices behind. In the interpretation by Robert Hale, 'solitary contemplation is that moment of entering into deepest *koinonia* and love with the ineffable God, to seek to fulfil more perfectly that first part of our Lord's commandment of love, to love God with our whole heart, mind, soul, strength'.[6] It is the solitary journey in faith that every pilgrim undertakes despite the existence of a group of pilgrims or a mass of people walking around them. For, despite a multitude or in solitude, there is a personal dialogue, a personal challenge and a deeply personal change. For example, during June 2016 I had the opportunity to pray at the Sri Harimandir Sahib Amritsar (known as the Golden Temple) in the Holy City of Amritsar, Punjab, India.[7] Sri Harimandir Sahib does not only represent the 'distinct identity, glory and heritage of the Sikhs' but it is also 'a symbol of human brotherhood and equality'.[8]

Within the Golden Temple 'everybody, irrespective of cast, creed or race can seek spiritual solace and religious fulfilment without any hindrance'.[9] For Guru Nanak, founder of Sikhism, according to Gurnam Singh Sanghera, 'advocates freedom, condemns oppression and subjugation, and fosters a religion of spirit which is universal in character'.[10] For I was reminded when I reflected on my prayer at the Sri Harimandir Sahib that the Sikh scriptures state very clearly: 'No one is my enemy, nor anyone is a stranger to me and I am the friend of all.'[11]

A young Sikh who had already attended prayers in the morning brought me to the temple. Shoes were left with an attendant, washing of the body took place, the head was covered, and my life companion and I joined hundreds of people who were descending on the carpets where pilgrims walked under the midday sun. We kissed the ground where sacred stones pointed to the Sikh memory of holy men, and we prayed together with those who were bathing under the sun. There were literally hundreds of people who went around praying, listening to music and drinking water while others were resting on the floor. Musicians were playing music, and holy men were reading scriptures and blessing pilgrims; however, I felt very much that this was my experience, an individual experience of togetherness with many others. There was no need for words or narratives as our feet were burning on the hot ground and the end of my trousers became wet with the water that surrounded our walk.[12] I prayed that I would learn that there is no enemy and no foe but that we are all a common humanity, and I felt in the heat of the day the strong presence of an Absolute as I tried to follow the guide, who was agile and managed to walk fast in the midst of the pilgrims. My life companion felt ill, and we needed to exit from the crowds collecting shoes and water to seek shelter from the noise and the crowd. This experience of the Sri Harimandir Sahib was my experience of a hermit among pilgrims, of a Christian among Sikhs, with their warmth and firmness of voice, with their joy and their devotion. On the following day, I met

Professor Dhillon, who took my hand and kept it in his for what seemed like forever, as we were both fellow pilgrims, both of us meeting for the first time, with lots in common. We were both human beings, and we had both experienced the protection of Sri Harimandir Sahib.[13]

There was no return from the movement that had started at my hermitage and that for unknown reasons had brought me and my life companion to Sri Harimandir Sahib. However, the knowledge we had acquired of Sri Harimandir Sahib had been experiential, and the togetherness of faith had been of silence and closeness. I had experienced the sacred space of the Sikhs, and in doing so I had been able to meet Sikhs by having some ritual experience in common. It is a fact I have visited many temples and many sacred places in my life, and each one of those experiences of the divine have changed my perception of other faiths and other pilgrims. Those from other faiths who have visited my hermitage have also experienced such changes in perception and in experience. Thus, once an individual has entered the cell and has committed hours to contemplation and prayer, there is no return because the possibility of experiencing God is all-encompassing as well as challenging and terrifying. The experience of places of prayer and devotion are common to all humanity, and in experiencing such moments we come together in a manner that is simple and human. After such encounters, we cannot return to the distrust of other faiths, because we have experienced a glimpse of the unity of the divine reality. We have been transformed beyond recognition into members of humanity without the occupational levels that divide us into caste, class and race.

I recognize that to explain such a journey from isolated prayer into a human togetherness with others requires a language that is closer to poetry and art rather than to reasonable propositions and textual exchanges. In many ways, it is the imagination that allows the human mind to foresee paths and ways which were not explored previously. I am very much reminded of the possibilities that were imagined by the Christian monks that opened and sustained the Shantivanam ashram after India's independence, namely Abbé Jules Monchanin (Swami Paramārūbyānanda, 1895–1957), Dom Henri Le Saux (Swami Abhishiktananda, 1910–1973) and Dom Bede Griffiths (Swami Dayananda, 1906-1993).[14] Their vision was the vision of hermits who recreated the world through their own search for the Absolute without many words and many buildings. Their imagination was of a divine encounter between human beings who acknowledged and chanted to the Absolute together. Thus, in a post-reflection by Raimon Panikkar, he outlined the possibilities and achievement of the contribution of monastic life in general, and eremitical life in particular, to the common journey of interfaith dialogue.[15] Panikkar argued that 'to speak of a Buddhist monk or a Hindu monk or a Jaina monk or a Christian monk does violence to the words. The Christian, the Buddhist, the Jaina…are only qualifications of the search for that centre, for that core that any monk seeks.'[16]

I offer within this work my own experience of an eremitic life that has brought me into deep communion with pilgrims of other faiths, sometimes through silence and the sharing of experiences, at other times through the mediation of a dividing space through virtual reality. It offers glimpses of an eremitic attempt to become one not only with Christians but with all other pilgrims, especially Hindus and Buddhists.[17] The foundations of Arunachala Hermitage in Anstruther, Scotland, and Nalanda Hermitage in Santiago, Chile, both in July 2014, have provided the possibility of a place where, even for a few minutes, Christians, Buddhists and Hindus have sat on the floor together in silence mindful of a common and shared journey. The importance of interfaith dialogue between monks has been at the forefront of this experience, and within such experience the centrality of silence. Behind this experience there is the realization that language and words provide a misunderstanding between practitioners and that the absoluteness of the Word and of canonical texts have also divided honest human beings who otherwise are on a common journey.[18] I outline in Chapter 3 some of these conversations and silences and my own road to silence. For it is through the sound of silence that interfaith dialogue starts and continues.

Language becomes a problem because this togetherness in prayer and contemplation, in togetherness and silence, requires the language of the heart, the language of a contemplative and mystical theology that does not find an adequate language of expression within the daily language of commerce, work and the markets. These difficulties are usually manifested in the honest and kind questions of others who ask me what I do, to which it is easy to reply: I pray. However, beyond that answer and the subsequent conversation, it is difficult to convey that prayer and contemplation in silence are not an occupation but a journey of love with God and with others. Thus, once I have spent time with God, I want to meet those who are praying within other religious traditions to pray with them, to kneel on the floor while they prostrate or stand. Ultimately, and as a result of this diverse prayer in a shared space, I feel an enormous love, devotion and responsibility for them. The commandment 'love thy neighbour' does not only extend to alms and charitable work but also to our love for others whom we don't know, who don't share our way of life, our ideas and aspirations, and who have a different philosophical or symbolic system of understanding their lives and their journeys.

In June 2016 I had the opportunity to meet with a Hindu family in Amritsar whose members are all involved in education and are currently attached to the Cascade Centre for Education in Amritsar.[19] Discussions on education and religion led to my asking about the Nobel laureate Tagore and discussions on poetry and artistic forms. While members of the family had not formally read the Upanishads, their language of conversation was closer to the Upanishads in short reflections about life and reality. Such language was expressed in the fact that poetry was regularly being written by father, son and daughter as an expression of everyday life and thought.[20] After a late breakfast and in the context of conversations on education, the daughter read some poems in public with everybody listening to express what her history was. She had written a poem to her parents ('From You to Me') that was framed and occupied one of the main walls within their living room. While I was with them the poem was taken down from the wall, read together and commented on by all those present. It expressed the sense that without the daughter her parents would not be a couple, thus expressing the opposite sense of most Western poems by a daughter who would tell her parents that without them she would not be there. I responded to the poem and read to them the first draft of the India Declaration on a Shared Humanity that had been written on the previous day after the visit to the Sri Harimandir Sahib.[21] Our encounter was that of human beings reading poetry and discussing commonalities, joys and sufferings of such a journey.

The enormous potential of poetry and aesthetic forms reflects the historical language of mysticism and metaphysical forms used by Teresa of Avila and John of the Cross, whereby their mystical experience of castles and crosses surpassed the rational and orderly understanding of religion assumed by their contemporaries. It is worth dwelling on poetry and aesthetic forms in the context of interfaith dialogue because, after silence and a first encounter between practitioners of different religions, the means of expressions used by those who are part of such encounters are not necessarily words used in daily life. For the common daily language has different and sometimes opposed contextual meanings within the sociocultural contexts in which Christianity and Hinduism are practised as symbolic ways of life. Thus poetry becomes an important language of dialogue, not only between practitioners of different faiths but for hermits who must express their mystical or spiritual experiences of life to others. For example, the Buddhist hermit Milarepa wrote thousands of poems while in the solitude of his cave, expressing the personal experiences that were taking place in his search for enlightenment. Poems and songs became for him a way of finding the path to the end of suffering.[22] Raimon Panikkar has emphasized this different language used by mysticism and therefore by those who live in contemplation and are expressing such a contemplative approach to interfaith dialogue. For Panikkar reminds us that 'the mystical discloses to us precisely that not all can be reduced to consciousness, that there is a dimension of the real irreducible to the *logos*'.[23]

Those who have explored different religious traditions have also found meaningful encounters and spiritual paths in the oral narratives in the genre of stories that give some teachings and the wisdom of life through them. For example, Jesuit Anthony de Mello SJ collected stories from different traditions in order to pursue spiritual growth and to help others to grow.[24] His method was to read the story several times, even in groups, but at the end its final instruction was 'create a silence within you and let the story reveal to you its inner depth and meaning'.[25] Thus in the story 'The Song of the Bird' he points to the punchline of the story: 'The words of the Master are not to be understood. They are to be listened to as one listens to the winds in the trees and the sound of the river and the song of the bird.'[26] This approach could be used to read the Upanishads and let the text speak about others and about a human togetherness.

FROM THE HERMITAGE TO THE RIVER

I note that, while popularly a hermit is perceived as somebody who does not see people, the outer looking of a hermit is always present, and I would argue particularly within an outer vision of a common journey with other religions. Among contemporary examples, since 2013 Pope Francis has been a refreshing example of a person who has gone out of the Vatican to meet other religious leaders, for example his journey to Cuba to meet Patriarch Bartholomew of Russia and to pray and be together with refugees who profess other faiths and other histories. Thus on 24 March 2016 Pope Francis journeyed to the Centre for Asylum Seekers at Castelnuovo di Porto, located 15 miles north of Rome, to celebrate the Mass of the Supper of the Lord during Maundy Thursday in Holy Week. Since the beginning of his pontificate in March 2013 and following his previous practices as archbishop of Buenos Aires, Pope Francis has left the Vatican on Maundy Thursday to be with those in prison, refugees and those rejected by their own societies.[27] During the liturgy of Maundy Thursday, it is customary that the main celebrant washes the feet of some of those attending the Eucharist as a sign of that precious memory of the Lord who washed the feet of the disciples. Pope Francis washed the feet of refugees. Some of them were Catholics, but there were also Muslims, Hindus and Copts. In a short homily he told them: 'Today as well, there are two gestures. All of us here, [coming] together – Muslims, Hindus, Catholics, Copts, Evangelicals – but [being] brothers, sons of the same God who want to live in peace.'[28] Pope Francis further suggested that there are different ways of expressing togetherness so that gestures sometimes speak louder than words.

For dialogue is no more than an expression of togetherness that begins with the simple act of exchanging a word, and holding hands in friendship. Thus the words by Pope Francis to the meeting of Christians and Muslims at the Vatican in May 2016:

> Dialogue is going out of ourselves, with a word to hear the word of the other. The two words meet, two thoughts meet. It is the first step of a journey. Following this meeting of the word, hearts meet and begin a dialogue of friendship which ends with holding hands. Word, hearts, hands. It's simple! A little child knows how to do it.[29]

The inclusiveness of Hindus and Muslims within the washing of the feet, and the gesture of washing feet in silence rather than through words, outline some of the basic content of a dialogue between those who follow a different religious path. This journey can sometimes be shared through words but most of the time can be shared with goodwill in the silence of a social togetherness. Thus, silence becomes essential to understand the language of those who have emphasized the communication with God and with one another in the context of dialogue. Among those who emphasize silence and solitude for the encounter with God and others are the hermits 'who devote their life to the praise of God and salvation of the world through a stricter separation from the world, the silence of solitude and assiduous prayer and penance'.[30]

THE WAY OF THE PILGRIM

I am a Catholic Benedictine hermit at the Hermitage of Arunachala who over the years has explored Buddhist and Hindu practices of meditation, philosophy and prayer within a life of contemplation and silence. At the same time in my life as a scholar I have explored issues of theological dialogue between Christianity, Buddhism and Hinduism, having stressed the textual and experiential knowledge of those Indian traditions. My visits to India for research and prayer have given me the possibility of exploring this dialogue with Buddhists and Hindus, and I have led attempts at interfaith dialogue with Hindus and Buddhists through the Centre for the Study of Religion and Politics (CSRP) of the University of St Andrews and fellow pilgrims in India who have been connected through the Arunachala Hermitage of Scotland and the Milarepa Foundation of Chile.

The history of Christian–Hindu dialogue in India started within contemporary space and time with the opening of the first Christian ashram in 1950 and with the residence in India of five pioneers of dialogue, all Catholic priests who became monastic ascetics in the line of Hindu *sadhus* and with an enormous influence of the school of *Advāita Vedānta*. Four pioneers, residing in India at the same time as the proceedings of Vatican II

(1962–1965), had an influence on the breath of dialogue and recognition of the sacredness of Hinduism within the Catholic Church.[31] Three of them belonged to the Benedictine monastic family and lived in India as Christians inspired by Hinduism. They were Abbé Jules Monchanin (1895–1957), Dom Henri Le Saux (1910–1973) and Dom Bede Griffiths (1906–1993).

However, less has been written about the life of hermits in Christianity and Hinduism. For, in both traditions, there are men and women who live a life of prayer and meditation in a hermitage that is neither part of a monastery nor a rule of consecrated life. In Hinduism, the *sanyasi* (renouncers) look for caves and solitary places to find the Self and the Absolute, while within Christianity there have been men and women who have followed the spirituality of the desert in rural or urban areas and those who have seen a model of solitary life and dialogue in the late Thomas Merton and have acquired traits of such solitude and interfaith dialogue.

Very little has been written about the actual organization of time and space, prayer and meditation that these hermits have conducted within these traditions. The experience of having to organize these spaces in time has made possible a deeper interfaith dialogue in which Christians and Hindus, and previously Buddhists, have prayed together and meditated together, finding a unifying chord in their dialogue which has been silent or spoken, localized or at a distance in a globalized community. For it is a human fact of life that buildings acquire a symbolic meaning assigned to them by others. Those buildings provide the possibility of meaning-charged or neutral spaces for the life and interaction of groups of humanity. Hermitages and hermits have in the line of interfaith dialogue a responsibility to create liminal spaces – sanctuaries in which human beings can find the meaning of a common humanity in times of peace or war. As a result, hermitages due to this creation of a liminal space become also liminal places in which a prophetic challenge to violence and disunity arises with the task, through prayer and meditation, to bear witness to the atrocities committed in the name of religion and of God. Thus, the possibility of forgetting the dead is not a possibility, because in forgetting the dead we kill them again.[32]

The spatial organization of a hermitage does not provide only the physical space where metaphysical activities can take place but a sanctuary at times in which to bear witness to the past becomes a challenge to ever-forgetting younger generations of fundamentalists, radicalized terrorists and hateful pseudo-followers of religious or philosophical movements. Within this reaffirmation of the witnessing to the past, a hermitage proclaims the great possibilities of the Kingdom, of a united humanity, of a Jerusalem in which all children of God of different faiths will arrive and live in peace. It is the utopic dreaming that embodies any following of the Absolute, the possibility that even after many reincarnations a human being can exit *samsara* regardless of the political implications of the immutable caste system. Thus, the radical commitment and assumed responsibility is not to forget others and, in the words of Rosemary Radford Ruether, to foster 'a quest for mutual justice between neighbours who must learn to live together in one land and one earth'.[33] Thus, in her analysis of Christian theologies and the Holocaust, she argued that 'this quest must curb the tendencies of all three monotheistic faiths to foster triumphalist self-affirmation through hatred and negation of others'.[34] And if a substantial reflexion of the Holocaust as a moment of darkest humanity and racism at its peak, the 1947 partition of India and the killing of Muslims and Hindus brings the possibility of a contemporary witness to the truth of death and of the dead who were killed in the name of religion.[35]

THIS WORK

This work includes rites, prayers and texts that I have used for interfaith dialogue at Arunachala Hermitage with the proviso that the best dialogue has been conducted in silence. Thus, the aim of Arunachala Hermitage is to welcome Christians, Hindus and Buddhists to come in silence to pray together and to dwell in the unity of the Absolute, the Trinity and Creation within the common tradition of prayer and contemplation. The liturgies mentioned and proposed in this work have been celebrated at Arunachala Hermitage in Anstruther and in India in the spirit of a common but diverse journey between Christians and Hindus.

Chapter 1 explores the lives of hermits of the twentieth century and their contribution not only to an eremitic life but to an ongoing witness to interfaith dialogue. In their own time and space they had to build their own places for contemplation in solitude, but in doing so they had the opportunity to foster contacts with people of other faiths.

Chapter 2 provides some spatial and theological reflections on how a single space can become a hermitage with an interfaith emphasis and an ongoing connection with Hinduism.

Chapter 3 explores the conversations in the context of interfaith dialogue between a Christian and a Hindu and the ramifications of a journey together within the context of a shared humanity.

Chapter 4 explores liturgies and prayers that can be used for Christian–Hindu dialogue and for a daily memorial of the journey together even when separated by geographical locations and ritual belongings.

Chapter 5 provides a textual commentary of a *lectio divina* using the Gospel of John and the Upanishads.

Chapter 6 is a meditation on the common journey of suffering and respect that leads to a meditation on death as a common human phenomenon and the challenges to comprehend the killing of innocent human beings in the name of an ethnic religion.

HERMITS IN CHRISTIANITY AND HINDUISM

It is five o'clock and the darkness covers the city of Santiago in winter. Even the other sentient beings at the hermitage, three budgies, do not attempt to face the possibility of an early morning meditation. Nalanda is located within a block of flats in the city centre, blocks away from the presidential palace. A Christian cross, a Buddhist tanka and a copy of the Upanishads convey the uniqueness of the place. And the morning starts with a silent meditation and a short reading of the Upanishads. From 5am to 8.30am the silence of the neighbourhood quietly rises into the noises of human beings starting their day. The day has started with a pointed meditation towards the Ganges where sadhus and pilgrims alike witnessed the beginning of the day with the fire ceremony. Hours of bliss in which the union of a prayer language goes beyond the possibilities of the duality of the spiritual and matter binding reality into the non-duality of a common language: that of silence, prayer, contemplation and meditation. By 8.30am coffee is being served with bread and jam and a bit of juice while the day lies ahead amongst the noises of birds and the possibility of human beings moving around. For it is that silence that remains the binding force within the daily activities that resemble the symphony of a humanity that stops its daily task of prayers and mantras in order to search for food, work and a shared humanity.

I am reminded of the words of Bede Griffiths who wrote 'what is required is a meeting of the different religious traditions at the deepest level of their experience of God'.[1] But for such experience to take place, a particular space within human time is needed, a space that can contain heaven and earth, and the thundering roars of a silence that does not belong to humanity but to the Absolute, to the eternal Trinity in its abode of silence.[2]

Within the eremitical experience of the twentieth century there have been a number of Christians who experienced the possibilities of a contemplative Christianity vis-à-vis other religions and their lives inspiring others not only to pursue a common path of understanding with people of other faiths but also to become hermits in the process. This chapter dwells on the historical tradition in order to examine some of the processes, tensions and lives experienced by Charles de Foucauld (1858-1916), Sadhu Sundar Singh (1889–1929), Thomas Merton (1915–1968) and Swami Abhishiktananda (1910–1973).[3] Their lives were marked not only by a daily search for the Absolute but also by their intense interaction with other faiths following the importance of silence, so that, in the words of Panikkar, all 'reality has an element of Silence'.[4] Their uniqueness lies in the possibilities they created to open avenues of interfaith, solitude and contemplation that had not been previously explored. They became guests and friends of followers of other religions, and in being guests they could recreate eremitical lives and humanly based interfaith encounters and conversations.

CHARLES DE FOUCAULD: EMBRACING POVERTY

Viscount Charles-Eugéne de Foucauld was born in Strasbourg on 15 September 1858 to a family of soldiers and priests who had served France for centuries.[5] The family motto 'Never Retreat' bore witness to the Foucaulds who had fought in the Crusades and who had stood beside Joan of Arc at Orleans. At the age of six Charles and his sister became orphans, and both of them were raised by their maternal grandparents. Charles joined the French cavalry at St Cyr and became part of the Fourth African Hussars fighting in Algeria and Morocco. His experience as an officer within these campaigns left him with a love for the silence and the open spaces of the desert. In 1883 he joined a rabbi in order to explore Morocco, conducting a geographical expedition that brought him honours and recognition by the geographical society of France. His encounter with Muslims and with Islam made a big impression on him, particularly the call for prayer and the prostrations made by hundreds of Muslims throughout the Moroccan desert. He thought of becoming a Muslim, and the sight of Muslims praying everywhere disturbed his previous understanding of life. His own spiritual journey was in a sense triggered by Islam, and when he returned to France he met a learned priest, Abbé Huvelin, who was to guide him in his confession of sins and his search for a deeper Christian life. Abbé Huvelin advised him to make a pilgrimage to the Holy Land, and when he returned he joined the Trappist Monastery of our Lady of the Snows. In 1891 he asked to be transferred to the poorest of the Trappist monasteries in Akbès, Syria. However, after seven years as a Trappist, he was released from his vows so as to follow his own vocation, and from 1897 to 1900 he worked as an unpaid servant of the Poor Clares in Nazareth and Jerusalem. He slept on the floor of a garden shed and lived an austere life of prayer and contemplation.

In 1901 he was ordained in France and decided to return to Algeria and to live at the oasis of Béni Abbès. With the help of French soldiers at the nearby garrison he built a hermitage made of mudbricks and palms, and he devoted himself to study and prayer, manual work and charity. He lived on bread, water and a few dates and slept curled on the floor in front of the altar. In 1905 he moved deep into the desert at Tamanrasset, a humble village in the Hoggar Mountains where the Tuareg lived.[6] He built a small hermitage made of stones and mud and decided to learn the Tuareg language and to prepare a Tamashegh grammar and dictionary as well as to collect some of their poems and sayings.[7] His approach to dialogue was clear, he took the first step, he made a point of playing with children, he visited the sick and welcomed at his hermitage a constant stream of visitors. His neighbours were 20 families, half way up a mountain at an altitude of 1400 metres (4600 feet).[8] In 1908 he received a dispensation from the Vatican to say Mass without a server and to keep the Eucharist in a self-built tabernacle.[9] However, on 1 December 1916 a group of about 40 rebels knocked at the door of the then fortified hermitage and took him out. As they were searching the hermitage, the sound of camels was heard, and the boy who was pointing his gun at him shot him dead.[10]

Was he a martyr for the faith or was he killed by mistake? Both are possible answers. He was a Christian who lived dangerously in the solitude of the Algerian desert and who despite the welcoming spirit of the Tuareg was French. The advent of the First World War and the French presence in Algeria could be deemed as factors that made the Sanusi rebels enemies of France and enemies of the unwelcomed French presence in Algeria.[11] However, he expected that he could be killed. Thus, within papers that he was carrying, there were writings that expressed his welcoming of martyrdom if it came. The verdict by Christian writers was that he was a holy person who followed the silent path of Jesus of Nazareth and wanted to live among Muslims. His great contribution to the development of an eremitic life and to interfaith dialogue was recognized not only by the Christian world but also by Ali Merad, a Muslim scholar.

In 1975 Merad, a professor of Arabic literature and civilization at the University of Lyon, published *Charles de Foucauld au regard de l'Islam.*[12] Merad makes a challenging contribution that does not fall within a scholarly work or try to answer why Muslims did not write about a man who lived among Muslims. Instead, his is 'an act of testimony', 'a testimony motivated by the desire to make a contribution, however small, to the Muslim–Christian dialogue'.[13] Merad admits that for over 20 years he has pondered the life of a Christian among Muslims, having been 'summoned' by the message of Charles de Foucauld.[14] Merad decides not to approve or condemn the actions of the 'Christian marabout' because, while acting within the sociopolitics of his time, he was 'a person consumed by an inner fire that was, for him, the love of Jesus and a passion for the imitation of Jesus'.[15]

Like his young friend Louis Massignon, the great French Arabicist who became a guest and friend of Islam, Charles de Foucauld became a guest of Islam and 'a mystical witness to Jesus before Islam'.[16] Charles de Foucauld's witness to Jesus was apparent to devout Muslims who understood the prophetic role of Jesus within the Muslim tradition and who, with Merad, understood the powerful sign of living in Tamanrasset while being French. It is clear from Merad's reflections that he saw the 'Christian marabout' as a renouncer, and that like the Tuareg he was deeply shocked and challenged by such material and personal renunciation. At the time of Charles de Foucauld's death, one of his great friends, the Tuareg chief Moussa ag Amastane, wrote to Charles' sister, Madame de Blic, expressing what a Tuareg cannot express, feelings of sorrow, in the following words: 'When I heard of the death of our friend, your brother Charles, my eyes closed; everything turned dark; I wept and shed many tears, and I am in deep mourning.'[17] For in the summer of 1910 the great *amenukal* of the Hoggar had travelled to France and had visited Charles' family, including his sister and brother-in-law.[18] Immediately on his return to Algiers he had sent a letter to Charles in which he acknowledged Charles' renunciation in the following words: 'I also saw your brother-in-law; I visited their gardens and their homes. And there you are in Tamanrasset, like a pauper!'[19]

The 'marabout friend of Jesus', as Charles was called by the Tuareg, had become their friend as well as their guest, not because he was considered a marabout but because the Christian hermit did not behave like a marabout. A marabout (*murābit*) was in Arabic originally a soldier attached to the guard of a frontier post and later a religious person dedicated to the defence of the borders of the Islamic empire; finally the name was used for a religious person who lives on his own – that is, a hermit. However, over time the marabout acquired important social status and power, because they could bless or curse those around them. Therefore, they used their influence to be served and kept rather than to serve others and as a result Islam. Charles had challenged this concept by serving the Tuareg, by cleaning their houses and tending to their children, their old and their sick. Thus interfaith dialogue at Tamanrasset had evolved out of the holiness of a hermit who had challenged the power of the marabout with his example of service and simplicity. Moussa ag Amastane wrote to Charles' sister after Charles' death: 'Charles the marabout has died not only for you, he has died for us too. May God have mercy on him, and may we meet him in Paradise.'[20]

During his time at Tamanrasset, Charles wrote a prospective rule for those who would join him in the same way of life. Within that text he put very clearly the total renunciation to be kept by others, as was the norm within religious congregations, particularly missionary ones. Charles stated that it would not be possible to receive any gifts, not even Mass offerings, offerings for prayers or for aiding the poor, and that the brothers would live only with the work of their hands. Further, he made the following provision against savings:

> In order to be charitable and to help the poor, we will keep no money from one week to the next. On Saturday, when the weekly pay is received, all money that is left over from the week before will be given to the poor. The same applies to provisions. Nothing will be kept from one week until the next.[21]

Thus, Charles' intended ascetics was a reflection on his own prophetic life centred in prayer within the world of the poor, so that, in the words of Ellsberg, 'he pioneered a new model of religious life, patterned after the life of Jesus himself, whose only cloister was the world of the poor'.[22]

The legacy of Charles de Foucauld for generations to come was his own sense of being a hermit that challenged the possibilities of following this vocation within larger institutions and certainly his prophetic challenge to the distance between Christianity and Islam. At a time in which a colonial power was still present in Algeria, this challenge was even more poignant. Those influenced by the desert as a place for hermits developed Charles' closeness to God and neighbour in the development of hermitages within the city. Carlo Carretto (1910–1988) and his *Letters from the Desert* particularly developed a unique sense that most Christians in their own places could create spaces for prayer and contemplation. In *The Desert in the City* Carretto argued that it was possible to recreate the desert in urban spaces and within busy lives.[23] Carretto was a member of the Little Brothers of Jesus, who showed that it was possible to live a contemplative life as a lay person and that an ascetic spirituality was also a joyful one.[24] Through Carretto a whole generation of young people in the 1980s became aware of the possibilities of the desert in their own working and professional lives.[25] However, the experience of Charles de Foucauld was lived by other Christians who searched for an eremitical life in the context of India and the interfaith experiences with Hinduism.

HERMITS IN THE INDIAN CONTEXT

India and Hinduism in general have a tradition of men and women who decide to renounce their lives and possessions to live an ascetic life. Those who renounce and live lives of personal ascetic practice and contemplation are certainly revered within India. For renunciation as such is not the most important factor but, as Panikkar has explained, it is the stripping of everything that creates social reverence because the renouncer is 'an example of a pure life stripped of everything'.[26] The renouncer's body, in Panikkar's understanding, 'exists in the pureness of the *ātman*, in the transparency of the *brahman*, in the surprising Presence of which the witnesses of the life of the holy man are more or less aware'.[27] For it is only when we do not desire something that we can renounce and become ascetics.

SRI RAMANA MAHARSHI

One of those ascetics who made an impression and affected Christian monasticism in India was the Bhagavān Ramana Maharshi, who advocated 'spiritual silence'. The Bhagavān was directly responsible for advancing the developments within the transformation of Abhishiktananda (Dom Henri Le Saux) from an ashram dweller to a *sanyasi* in northern India. Sri Ramana Maharshi was born on 29 December 1879 in Tiruchuzhi, a small town in Tamil Nadu, on the day when the town was celebrating the festival of Arudra Darshan.[28] The festival commemorates the apparition of the god Siva as Nataraja in the cosmic dance of creation. Within the festival the image of Siva garlanded with flowers is taken through the town during the day and especially at night, accompanied by the sound of the drums and the conches amidst the chanting of its devotees. On that day and at dawn the image was taken back to the temple while Maharshi was born to a town's accountant clerk, Sundaram Ayyar, and his wife, Alagammal. The baby was named Venkataraman, to be later revered as an embodiment of Siva with the name Sri Ramana Maharshi. As he grew older, Maharshi developed a great joy and a fascination with the fact that the Holy Mountain of Arunachala was so close. However, he had a moment of 'awakening', as it is known in Sanskrit, in which he felt the awakening of the self. Maharshi was 17, and he had already felt a current of awareness, but in one moment he felt an enormous fear of death.

He laid down with arms outstretched and realized that if death were to come only the Self would remain as a manifestation of Brahma. It is unusual for a person to realize the Self without a long journey, but in the case of Maharshi this realization was recognized by many.

The 'Preface' to his collected works makes quite clear what the meaning of this realization was:

> to say that the Maharshi realized the Self does not mean that he understood any new doctrine or theory or achieved any higher state or miraculous powers, but that the 'I' who understands or does not understand doctrine and who possesses or does not possess powers became consciously identical with the Atman, the universal Self or Spirit.[29]

Maharshi had his first Western disciple in 1911, a high-ranking policeman of the Madras police force.[30] In the 1950s he became well known in Western circles through Paul Brunton's *A Search in Secret India*, and the guru character taken from Maharshi's life was used in Somerset Maugham's *The Razor's Edge*.[31]

The writings of Maharshi were very few, mostly triggered by requests to write his thoughts down, because his sense of learning was not through theory but through experience. Maharshi answered every question from his disciples and followers by returning the person who asked the question to his own Self-knowledge, 'by which is not meant any psychological study but knowing and being the Self which exists behind the ego or mind'.[32] This search for Self-knowledge was to be a spiritual journey and a spiritual quest, and Maharshi's method of teaching was 'spiritual silence' in which he led his disciples to search for their Self-knowledge.

His collected works, edited by Arthur Osborne, reflected Maharshi's own chronology of the spiritual journey as he ordered them for a devotee who had a private collection of his writings. *Self-Enquiry* appears in this collection as the first and the most important work and method, a work that had been written by Maharshi in 1901, when he was 22 years old. Maharshi had already realized his Self and was living, mostly in silence, in Virupaksha cave on the hill of Arunachala. Disciples gathered around the cave and one of them, Gambhiram Seshayya, asked for his guidance. As Maharshi was in silence, he proceeded to write his instructions regarding 'self-enquiry' and the path towards realization of the Self as well as instructions on a meditation on one's identity with the Self and yogi exercises of breath control.[33] For Maharshi the quest for the Self was the quest to be transformed into the Self, because, in his words, 'from ignorance sprang the ego – the subtle body' so that 'the mind must be transformed into the Self'.[34] *Self-Enquiry* presupposed some knowledge of science. Thus, respiratory exercises were described as spiritual exercises of self-purification which involve the understanding of the shared knowledge whereby on breathing all human beings shared the knowledge of the Absolute. For it is the Absolute that breathes life into every being that becomes in turn part of the divine essence. For Maharshi 'the ego in the form of the "I-thought" is the root of the tree of illusion, its destruction fells illusion', and the whole method of ego-destruction is called *bhakti* (devotion), *jnana* (knowledge), *yoga* (union) or *dhyana* (meditation).[35] The vedantic doctrine that postulates One Supreme Reality, dismissing the names and forms of all else as illusion, permeated this knowledge of the Self. Maharshi also rejected the idea of 'the One Creating, Sustaining, and Absorbing Supreme Self as the separate gods, Ganapathi, Brahman, Vishnu, Rudra, Maheswara, and Sadasiva'.[36] The whole truth for Maharshi was expressed in 'Worship Is Only Self-Enquiry':

> The body is not I. Who am I? Enquire in this way, turning the mind backward to its primal state. The enquiry 'Who am I?' is the only method of putting an end to all misery and ushering in supreme Beatitude. Whatever may be said and however phrased, this is the whole truth in a nutshell.[37]

For Maharshi the point where there is no beyond between the liberated Self and the Absolute is reached through constant meditation in which the Absolute and the negation of the body are experienced at times until they become one. Most people attain liberation after death and immortality remains a possibility, but those who follow the right path of constant meditation can attain liberation within this life, so that 'he who experiences that Bliss is liberated even when still alive'.[38] For those who had difficulties with meditation, Maharshi prescribed yoga in order to attain a path towards liberation, and one of those disciplines within yoga made a real impact on Abhishiktananda: the *pravana* or recitation of the AUM (OM). The *pravana* is the incantation of OM with three and a half beats: A, U and M, and a half beat of M.[39] A refers to the waking state, the gross body and creation; U refers to the dream state, the subtle body and preservation; M refers to deep sleep, the Self at rest in sleep, the causal body and dissolution; and finally, the fourth state, the half sound, stands for the true state of the I or Self with only one possibility beyond: Bliss. The half sound provides the sub-divisions of all sounds and it is known as 'silent incantation' and 'non-dual incantation' – the essence of all incantations.[40] In summary, all forms of meditation prepare for this ultimate meditation on the Self so that:

> knowing one's own Self is knowing God. Not knowing the nature of him who meditates but meditating on God as foreign to one's own Self is like measuring one's shadow with one's foot. You go on measuring while the shadow also goes on receding further and further.[41]

The end of *Self-Enquiry* concerns itself with renunciation (*sannyāsa*), as a renunciation not of material or external things but renunciation of the ego. For a *sanyasi*, he who renounces, there is no difference between solitude and active life, so that the *sanyasi*, even when engaged in external work, is not the doer, 'because his mind is immersed in the Self without the uprising of the ego'.[42]

All other works by Maharshi returned to the basic explanations and teachings expanded in *Self-Enquiry*.[43] *Who Am I?* (Nan Yar) was written at the same time as *Self-Enquiry* as a response to 14 questions posed by Sivaprakasam Pillai, one of Maharshi's early disciples.[44] It is important to understand that Abhishiktananda heard these teachings and received transmissions from Maharshi's devotees. Maharshi's written texts were not available at that time, and the whole point of learning from a guru was to listen and to be with somebody who had lived the principles and the way of liberation. Because of that life according to the principles that led to liberation, he could guide others. Following from these demands by his disciples, Maharshi composed five hymns to Arunachala, written around 1914, when he was 35 years of age. He was staying at a cave, and some of the *sadhus* who were receiving his teachings asked him to compose some songs that they could sing on their daily walk to Tiruvannamalai, where they begged for alms and food. While Maharshi rejected the idea at the beginning, he composed the hymns later. The first hymn, 'The Marital Garland of Letters', was composed while he walked around the hill praising the love and union between the human soul and God.[45] One can imagine the power and emotion experienced by the *sadhus* who walked chanting the final chorus of the Marital Garland: 'Oh Arunachala! My Loving Lord! Throw Thy garland [about my shoulders], wearing Thyself this one [strung] by me, Arunachala!'[46] The second, third and fourth hymns were poems that he composed spontaneously. He also composed the *Eleven Stanzas to Sri Arunachala* at one per day and the *Eight Stanzas to Sri Arunachala*. They were words that came to him, that he tried to ignore, and that finally he wrote down one at a time. As he was walking around the hill his disciple Palaniswami carried with him paper and pencil, and as soon as Maharshi wrote a stanza, he sent it to town to be typed and printed. The fifth hymn came about when the Sanskrit poet and devotee Ganapati Sastri asked Maharshi to write a poem in Sanskrit. Maharshi usually wrote in Tamil, and he suggested that he didn't know how to write a stanza in Sanskrit. However, after Sastri explained to him how to construct a Sanskrit poem, Maharshi wrote one with some difficulty, and after some unexpected words the path to realization came to him.

In all these writings Maharshi associated the word Arunachala with God and also with the sacred hill where he lived most of his life. It was this association with the hill that Abhishiktananda found quite meaningful for his own path to God, because it had been at the caves of Arunachala that Abhishiktananda had experienced silence, renunciation and a deep sense of what India had to offer him as a contemplative. Arunachala became one of the many spiritual centres of India precisely because of Maharshi's ashram and his teaching that came to be identified with the Hindu school of *advāita* and self-enquiry. For Maharshi, Arunachala was the place where he continued his self-enquiry, not having had a guru to teach him. This unusual path of self-realization without a guru was explained by him suggesting that sometimes a guru does not necessarily take human form even when he is not opposed to learning from a guru. Thus, in 'The Glory of Sri Arunachala', he suggested that 'the true import of the Vedanta... is easily attained by all who can either directly sight this Hill or even mentally think of it from afar'.[47] Further, in 'The Necklet of Nine Gems', Maharshi confessed, 'Oh Arunachala! As soon as Thou didst claim me, my body and soul were Thine.'[48] However, the hymns also expressed some connections between the Self, God and an ongoing search when Maharshi wrote, 'Arunachala, Supreme Self! Think no more to keep me at a distance from Thy Feet!'[49] Further, 'Thou art Thyself the One Being, ever aware as the self-luminous Heart!'[50] As his teachings progressed, and probably being tired of so many pilgrims who wanted a guru rather than the simple attainment of liberation by examining the Self, Maharshi re-emphasized that all paths including meditation, meditation techniques and prayers were only initial paths to the sole experience of *advāita*, the non-duality in which the Self and the Absolute become one.

SADHU SUNDAR SINGH

Among those Christian hermits who devoted their life to a way of silence, prayer and solitude in the Indian context, there was the central prophetic example of Swami Abhishiktananda, but there had also been Sadhu Sundar Singh in the early twentieth century. Born on 3 September 1889 in Rampur, a village in the Punjab, Sundar Singh belonged to an affluent Sikh family.[51] He attended a Methodist missionary school and was baptized at the age of 16 in Simla. Thirty-three days later he became an itinerant *sadhu*, talking about Christ, dressed in his saffron robes and his turban.

His upbringing had been within a Sikh family that also had deep respect for the Hindu Scriptures. As a child he was educated in the Vedas and the Guru Granth Sahib. He claimed to have a vision of Christ and decided to become a Christian, bringing shame to his family. The only Christians in the village cleaned houses and ate from the scraps left for them; they were outcasts, and Sundar's family were not very pleased that he wanted to become an outcast. As a declaration of his rejection of the Sikh religion he cut his long hair, and his family made him sleep on the veranda, outside the family boundaries. When he left home, he took the saffron robes. However, it has to be said that he maintained his deep respect for the religious traditions he had grown up with – that is, Hinduism, Buddhism, Sikhism and Islam.[52] He started an ongoing pilgrimage meeting the poor and the outcasts, and in his condition of a *sadhu* being welcomed by some of the rich as well. On return to his village he found that as a barefooted *sadhu* he was made welcome.

From the hills of Simla he could sense that he was close to the snows of Tibet, and his wish was always to visit Tibet. Thus in 1908 he crossed the snows into Tibet and was rejected because he was told that holy men never washed as he did. From 1912 onwards he visited Tibet regularly. He also visited Kailash, the holy mountain for the Hindus. He visited the renouncers and ascetics in the caves and was welcomed by some and stoned by others. In 1913 he returned from Tibet and went to Haridwar on the Ganges, where he fasted for 40 days. After recovering from the fast he continued visiting India, Tibet and Nepal until 1919, when he visited China, Malaysia and Japan. In January 1920, and helped by his father, he sailed from Bombay to Europe in order to see the life of materialism in Europe. He filled halls and parish churches where he spoke, and was even invited to visit European countries. Thus, in 1922 he spoke in Geneva, Oxford, London and Paris, as well as cities in Germany, Holland, Sweden, Norway and Denmark.

When he returned to India, he suffered from ill-health, and it was only in 1927 that he attempted to cross again from India into Tibet. However, he started bleeding during his attempt and was left behind by some railway workers. Two years later, in 1929, he crossed into Tibet but was never seen again. He was not a writer ordinarily, but wrote six slim books in the last years of his life in order to fulfil requests from friends and followers.[53] The first book was written in Urdu, his mother tongue, the others in English.[54]

It is clear that within the life of Sadhu Sundar Singh one can find the contradictions of a search for God at a time of colonial Christianity and rigid divisions of religion, caste and social grouping. Within those difficult social parameters of understanding, Sadhu Sundar explored an individual search for God as a wandering *sadhu* and hermit who came into contact with other religions, including Tibetan Buddhism. Within his eremitic and spiritual challenge there was a personal critique of Europe and a European colonial Christianity of the establishment. He was a pioneer of Christian forms of life which were, during the twentieth century, to look more kindly and with some excitement towards metaphysical understandings within Hinduism. One of those who continued this kind of critique of colonial Christianity from within was a French Benedictine, Dom Henri Le Saux, later to be known as Swami Abhishiktananda.

SWAMI ABHISHIKTANANDA

On 27 August 1968 Abhishiktananda left Shantivanam Ashram and had the chance to advance his own solitary life at his *kutiya* at Gyansu, a place beside the Ganges made up of a small collection of temporary dwellings, one kilometre (0.6 miles) from Uttakarshi. From 1969 to 1971 he spent six to eight months every year in solitude and for the rest of the year gave talks or visited friends, as his presence by others exploring Christianity and Hinduism was in great demand. His heart attack in July 1973 interrupted his residence at Gyansu after he had spent only four months in solitude between 1972 and 1973. During 1972 Abhishiktananda was away for an operation and at the same time took care of Marc Chaduc, his first and only disciple, who being a Frenchman did not have a government permit to reside at Gyansu. Thus, Abhishiktananda had to leave Gyansu periodically in order to meet him.

Abhishiktananda's relocation to northern India had three important moments in his development of a Christian–Hindu dialogue: his own personal prayer and meditation with an increasing awareness of *advāita* and *sannyāsa*; his involvement with the All-India Seminar at Bangalore and the post-Vatican II liturgical developments within India; and his role as a master to one disciple whom he loved.

In his own personal prayer and meditation Abhishiktananda started developing forms of liturgical developments in which he could explore the possibilities of incorporating further Hindu readings and ways of prayer. He had written previously about an 'acosmic being' as the prototype of a Christian *sanyasi*, and he was hopeful that his move to Gyansu would provide an opportunity of living as an 'acosmic being' in his own life.[55] Thus, he wrote that '[*advāita*] takes a man out of himself, in order to bring him to his fullness as a man. Is that not the deep meaning of the Resurrection? Everything dies, but everything is reborn.'[56] Abhishiktananda was not fully convinced that the new liturgical rites developed after Vatican II and that came into use in 1972 were made for India. He saw the difficulties of bringing together the Patristic tradition, the Vedantic tradition and the contemporary language of the post-Vatican II era. In developing such liturgical outcomes, Abhishiktananda continued studying and discussing the Upanishads with others. In November 1968 he went to Jyotiniketan Ashram for another session of study of the Upanishads, sessions in which Sr Térese and Maria Bidoli, an Italian research student staying at Varanasi, took part. The sessions were combined with studies of the Bible at a time when Sr Térese was thinking of settling in Allahabad.

Abhishiktananda was conducting liturgical experiments within his daily celebration of the liturgy. He was very conscious that he would become just a collector of data if he didn't advance his own ways of advancing a Christian–Hindu encounter. He mentioned that after many experiments on a Sanskrit liturgy he was advancing a liturgy for a Free Church (an expression that he took from Murray Rogers). Daily, Abhishiktananda composed a different Canon for the morning Mass during the previous evening before going to sleep. His stay at Jyotiniketan allowed him to share some of these experiments with others who were also studying the Upanishads.[57] The morning celebration included readings and chants from the Hindu scriptures and a homily on the Gospel of the day. Other variations in hymns and readings related to the possible variations in daily life of Hindu communities around them. For example, Abhishiktananda recalled that when their Hindu neighbours had a festival in the river they read a hymn to the Waters from the Rig Veda, Isaiah 50 and John 4. On the day of the saints of the Benedictine Order (13 November) they remembered in prayer and thanksgiving all the saints and holy monks of every tradition.[58]

The main celebrant in these liturgical experiments came from the different Christian traditions – thus one day Abhishiktananda presided, while on the following day Murray Rogers presided. Abhishiktananda expanded the 'Preface' to include all bishops and priests of Rome and Constantinople, while texts for the first part of the Canon included John 1.1–14 and 13.1.[59] One of Abhishiktananda's realizations that was to solve his own interior tension between Christianity and Hinduism was that 'the tension between Vedanta and Christianity is insoluble. I tried to go beyond it in *Sagesse*. The last chapter shows that I was unable to do so.'[60] Abhishiktananda's explanation for this limitation is that we try to judge experiences conceptually from the outside. He preferred a long Mass of more than an hour with an abundant use of Indian texts, assuming that the only support in a collapsing European theology is the Hindu discovery of 'I am'.[61] He returned to Jyotiniketan for Holy Week 1969, and some of his experimental additions of Indian texts were added to the liturgy. For example, the fire for the Paschal Vigil, a *homa*, sacred fire, was lit outside before taking the new fire into the Church, and the reading of Genesis 1 was preceded by the reading of Rig Veda 10.21 as a hymn of praise to the Creator. After Easter he went to Allahabad to check his Sanskrit Mass and Canon with a Hindu *pandit*.

As well as these ecumenical experimentations, Abhishiktananda appreciated the possibilities offered by the All-India Seminar, which was to discuss the actual implementation of Vatican II in India and that was to take place in Bangalore. Thus, after his stay at Jyotiniketan, he went to Varanasi to discuss the All-India Seminar with Raimon Panikkar and to Agra, where he took part in a regional seminar that was preparing the All-India Seminar. He discovered that the Bishop of Banaras had attached his name to the list of delegates going to Agra.[62] Within the discussions at Agra two out of the four bishops were not happy about the theme of dialogue and were quickly reminded by one of the speakers that if they thought dialogue was not a theme they would forget what Vatican II had said and their task to implement the council in India and in every Catholic diocese of India. The liturgical experimentation that had started positively with the 'Indian Mass' at Poona had created a heated correspondence in the *Examiner*, and the Bishop of Bangalore had ended any semi-public experimentation on an Indian liturgy.[63] Despite those disputes, in March 1969 Abhishiktananda started work in earnest for the All-India Seminar, proof-reading two books that were to be his own contribution to the Seminar.[64] At the end of March he was working with the team preparing the handbook for the spirituality workshop at the Seminar, and he agreed to become a member of the spirituality workshop in the section devoted to 'integrating Indian values in Christian spirituality'. Part of his concern was to have a 'pilot group' at some Catholic seminaries and he visited Ranchi, Allahabad and Delhi.

The All-India Seminar took place in Dharmaram College, Bangalore, from 15 to 25 May 1969.[65] Abhishiktananda made an important contribution within the spirituality workshop, his books were on sale and he was in demand because other seminar groups needed his input. He worked particularly with a group of priests of the Carmelites of Mary Immaculate from Kerala who had been encouraged by their Bishop Cardinal Parecattil on the development of an Indian liturgy for the Syro-Malabar rite.[66] He fought actively for amendments of texts that could integrate the contemplative dimension into the liturgical life of India and he made a tremendous impression.[67] On a more personal basis he wrote, 'I got very large majorities for two amendments, one calling for ashrams of "pure prayer and silence", the other for a liturgical renewal in depth, drawing on the values of Indian interiority.'[68] Abhishiktananda was quite happy about the All-India Seminar and it went beyond his expectations particularly because of the way in which the Indian bishops discussed issues of the church in India with everybody else. However, he also wanted a quick implementation on issues of silence and prayer and he suggested that 'what we shall need even more will be the formulation of a basic theology to undergird this renewal – the place of non-Biblical traditions in the Salvation History'.[69] On his way back from Bangalore, Abhishiktananda stopped in Bombay to join a group of young Jesuits and novices of the Sacred Heart (RSCJ) who were celebrating a week of spirituality. He had the opportunity to celebrate the Mass Indian-style, to their delight, and he was glowing with hope for the Church in India.

From June to October 1969 Abhishiktananda remained in Gyansu. During those three and a half months he planted a vegetable garden and employed a boy to cook his lunch, which daily consisted of rice, split peas, potatoes and marrow – all cooked together – and half a litre of milk. He wrote several papers and started his work on the implementation of the Seminar. However, his first and central concern was that of a theology in which Europe and the East could meet. He felt that without a theology of dialogue and encounter all the activities on prayer and meditation would only remain activities. Thus, he wrote: 'the problem of Christianity–Vedanta is crucial – much more so than the problem of Christianity–Humanism'.[70] His thoughts were shared only with Raimon Panikkar, who in his *The Unknown Christ of Hinduism* had developed a similarity in incarnation in Christianity and Hinduism, Christ and Iśvara, fulfilling an identical role in the two systems.[71] In a letter to Panikkar, Abhishiktananda agreed with this interpretation and radically argued that 'Christ shares the transitoriness of the world of manifestation, of *māyā*', so that 'whoever, in his personal experience…has discovered the Self, has no need of faith in Christ, of prayer, of the communion of the Church…' However, Abhishiktananda posed a clear difficult question to the centrality of Christ and the catholicity of the Church, if such experience of manifestation cannot be expressed in Indian terms:

> What is the meaning of this unique Son of God? For an *advāitin anubhavī* [one who has experience of *advāita*] Christ can only be the ideal in human terms (i.e. at the level of manifestation) who has best actualized the mystery and the experience of the AHAM [I] which is no two![72]

Abhishiktananda's letters from his solitude reflected his own spiritual and theological development. On the one hand, his great tension and desire to infuse his life with Christianity and Hinduism had been resolved by suggesting that there was no solution to such tension but in the centrality of God; on the other hand his involvement with Hindu practices had provided the fruits of liturgical diversity that he found in the past so difficult and had also given him the capacity to experience the all-encompassing centrality of the OM: 'OM. This eternal word is all: what was, what is and what shall be, and what beyond is in eternity. All is OM.'[73] Abhishiktananda the *sanyasi* had renounced his thought and his tradition.

THOMAS MERTON

During 1968, and as Abhishiktananda was searching for a new eremitic life beside the Ganges, another pioneer of the eremitic life and interfaith, Thomas Merton, arrived for a brief visit to India.[74] Merton had been given permission to attend a meeting of Benedictine and Cistercian Catholic abbots in Bangkok that had been organized by Aide à l'Implantation Monastique, a Benedictine international group that fostered the renewal of the monastic life.[75] Merton had taken the opportunity to visit India and to visit some of the foundational places for Hinduism and Buddhism as well as to meet three times with the 14th Dalai Lama. However, these developments had come about because years before Merton had decided to live in a small bungalow within the premises of the Abbey of Gethsemani as a hermit.

On 20 August 1965, on the Feast of St Bernard, Merton bid farewell to the monastery enclosure with an address with the title 'A life free from care'.[76] His novices gave him funny presents and cards, and later he went to collect the necessary supplies including ragged clothing. Every day he went to the abbey to say Mass in the library chapel and to eat one meal, usually on his own in the refectory of the abbey's infirmary. Regardless of a day of fasting or a day of work, Merton enjoyed one meal that kept him going.[77] His sole obligation was to give a conference every Sunday afternoon, and the abbot had requested that he write a revised manual for postulants. He had what he wanted, but after a week he started feeling lonely in the midst of manual work in the fields that he loved so much and a certain amount of daily writing, an activity that Michael Mott has correctly described rather as 'a compulsion than either a vocation or a job'.[78]

Merton's diaries do not carry a detailed description of his daily routines or timetables, only of readings he was doing, writings he enjoyed and comments on nature, the changing seasons or the weather. However, he described his daily life as a hermit to the Pakistani Sufi scholar Abdul Aziz, with whom he corresponded at a time in which Merton explored Islam and particularly the idea of community, prayer and purity.[79] Aziz had written to Merton on 1 November 1960 impressed by Merton's *The Ascent to Truth* and encouraged by another of Merton's friends, Louis Massignon. Both corresponded until 1968, and it was at the request of Aziz that Merton described his daily routine and his understanding and practice of prayer.[80] Thus, Merton described going to bed at 7.30pm and rising at 2.30am, followed by praying the office, meditation and Bible reading (*lectio divina*). Then he prepared tea or coffee and read until sunrise. At sunrise, Merton said morning prayer and then started manual work until 9.00am and wrote a few letters. Then he went to the monastery to say Mass and ate his only cooked meal of the day. At the time, he was writing to Aziz that he had not been authorized to say Mass in the hermitage, because in the pre-1972 rite he still needed an altar boy, etc. After the meal Merton returned to the hermitage, read and said the office at 1.00pm. After saying the office Merton meditated for another hour and then did some writing for a maximum of two hours. At 4.00pm he said another part of the office, followed by a light supper, mainly tea, soup and a sandwich. After supper he meditated for another hour or two and then went to bed.[81]

The letter to Aziz constitutes a unique description, because it shows a clear monastic timetable with little time for writing and correspondence, activities that dominated Merton's life. Merton recognized that he had a hard time keeping to this timetable and was very conscious that time passed very fast in the hermitage.[82] His pastimes were walks around the woods and the contemplation of nature and the use of a music player that allowed him to listen to music that other people regularly sent him, particularly jazz and contemporary songs related to the peace movement and the 1960s criticism of authority, including songs by Joan Baez and Bob Dylan.[83] He also enjoyed listening to some Mozart quintets as well, while recognizing that he was not into music as he had been in the previous years.[84]

His notes and comments on nature were beautifully written and showed a deep enjoyment of his own personal engagement with God's creation around him. For example, he wrote: 'The morning was dark, with a harder bluer darkness than yesterday. The hills stood out stark and black, the pines were black over thin pale sheets of snow. A more interesting and tougher murkiness.'[85] The change of seasons and the snow captivated him, and his comments were of an expectant child living a new and exciting experience, as in comments such as 'it is turning into the most brilliant of winters'.[86]

Merton almost never spoke about his own practice of prayer or of his relation with God, but he made an exception in the correspondence with Abdul Aziz, who received long and detailed descriptions of Merton's way of prayer and his understanding of God. The rubric of this correspondence outlines Merton's privacy regarding his own prayer movements when he warned Abdul Aziz, saying, 'I do not ordinarily write about such things and ask you therefore to be discreet about it.'[87] Merton's description of his prayer was simple and direct and he wrote, 'It is centred entirely on attention to the presence of God and to His will and His love. That is to say that it is centred on *faith* by which alone we can know the presence of God.'[88]

A PHILOSOPHY OF SOLITUDE

The historical and biographical aspects of Thomas Merton's life as a hermit have been outlined in his diaries and his letters; however, those writings contained little of what Merton thought about his time alone, his own reflection on the aspects of solitude that constituted a Christian charisma, and the centrality of solitude in the search for a purposeful desert.[89] For it is possible to argue that solitude can be sought for personal gain. This gain can have many aspects such as the gain of tranquillity, independence from others or a personal self-fulfilment in doing whatever one always wanted to do without explaining it to others. In the case of Merton, his search for the monastic life, for the eremitic life within a monastery, and his search for personal solitude, responded to his own search for a closer and fuller encounter with God.

Merton wrote about solitude in his 30-page essay 'Notes for a Philosophy of Solitude' (1960) in which he elaborated previous arguments defending monasticism and eremitism.[90] The important and crucial contribution of the 'Notes' lies in the fact that he extended his thoughts and reflections on solitude to lay people. The three main sections, 'The Tyranny of Diversion', 'In the Sea of Perils' and 'Spiritual Poverty', clearly located monasticism and solitude within a larger Christian vocation and thoughts of solitude with God as part of the charisma of the universal church and not solely of a chosen few.

In the section 'The Tyranny of Diversion' Merton argues that every human being is a solitary in the existential sense and that if this has not been realized in personal awareness it is because noises and activities of the world have impeded that self-realization of being, of Self, of solitude. Among those diversions there are central activities that numb the person in solitude, activities such as the amazement of money, the satisfaction of acquiring status and the justification of our own existence despite the existence of others within humanity. A person who lives through those diversions is not alienated from the world as she fits too well in society, but the diversions impede her from appreciating her true worth as a person in solitude. Thus every human being is a distinct person in solitude and not a single part in a larger community structure. Once the diversions disappear, there is a confusion rather than personal assertion, but it is through this process of confusion that God appears and helps restore the self-awareness of one's solitude within a larger busy and noisy world. This confusion requires faith in order to accept God's action and, in my view, differentiates Merton's idea of solitude from any other process of enlightenment or self-discovery.

This model and understanding of solitude was proposed for everybody within the church and it was published in advance of the reforms proposed by Vatican II that were to bring a significant change in the understanding of church. In the second section, 'In the Sea of Perils', Merton outlines the fact that the solitary is not fleeing society but transcending it, bringing new values that make society as it was obsolete. The solitary renounces everything that does not transcend and as a result renounces the short-lived illusions of diversion. However, the solitary does not live a personal dream of individualism but a challenge to the diversions offered by a society in which the transcendent does not have a place. For Merton the individualist world is not the desert but the womb. Instead, for the solitary, the loneliness that takes place is not the loneliness of the individual but the loneliness of God. The hermit then is for Merton a witness, a silent witness to a profound truth: the presence of God. Contemplation for a hermit does not become an esoteric exercise or realization but an awareness of the presence of God, in sympathy with others, that becomes a profound act of love, filled with the love of God. There is a clear distinction here from the metaphysics of cognition in Christian spirituality that borrows from Greek thought; instead, Merton dwells in and develops a way of contemplation and solitude that later would lead him into a presence of emptiness. Thus, Merton connected with the Christian mystics of the West as well as with the contemplative schools of the East symbolized through his study of Zen contemplation and emptiness.[91]

For Merton, contemplation and the act of solitude is an act of action because it expresses love and points towards the source of love: God. The contemplative and the solitary withdraw from the world, not in order to escape the world, but to heal it through an act of love and communication of the solitary with God, taking into solitude the world as it is, in need of transcendence and in need of love. A further characteristic of Merton's treatise on solitude is that, for him, the perfect solitude is not always expressed by the institutional life of the Carthusians or the Camaldolese but by those who have been chosen by solitude and who through the hard way have been drawn by solitude to experience the love of God in that solitude. Those who are chosen by solitude experience disillusionment and hardship and become true solitaries with God, because they have completely lost the illusion that the world is trying to give them and have found themselves solely in God.

One has to ask if Merton was speaking about his own situation as a monk and contemplative at the Abbey of Gethsemani. Thus, Merton's description of the true hermit in the second part of the essay refers to a harsh experience of spirituality, in that a hermit becomes a metaphor and an example of all Christians, because the hermit's encounter with God is the necessary experience of all Christians who at one point or another need to confront God face to face and alone. For Merton asserts once and again that the cenobitic life, the life in community that is lived by the Cistercians, is a proclamation of death to the values of the world but contradicts the life of a solitary hermit. The hermit in poverty and humility leaves the concern for community safety and in poverty shows sympathy to other human beings while confronting God alone, following every moment of silence as a path to God.

Thus, in part three of his 'Notes', within a section on 'Spiritual Poverty', Merton introduces the characteristics of the solitary as a person searching for solitude with God but with the frustrations and insecurities of every human being. The solitary life is God's will even when others have not reached this realization. For the solitary, life speaks of 'a common humanity' in which all are solitary and in need of God, a solitude that leads to 'compassion' and to a final break of distinctions of what belongs to one person or another. Here in these thoughts of part three, and within the use of 'a common humanity' and 'compassion', one can see the seeds of commonality with the spirituality and the tenets of Tibetan Buddhism. Those common ideas on contemplation and solitude were to create rapport between Merton and the 14th Dalai Lama in their encounter in India at the end of 1968.[92]

Merton outlined the difference between an 'I' of individualism that can be cultivated and the 'I' of the spirit that can only be and act. This solitary 'I' comes from God because it is through this 'I' that a human being encounters God who is another solitary 'I'. The gift of solitude is a gift of the spirit, and the sacramental manifestation of the encounter between a solitary soul and God is Christ himself, God manifested and incarnate.

CONSTRUCTING AN EREMITIC LIFE

It becomes clear from the lives of hermits outlined within this chapter that there is no one single rule for a hermit and that the individual search for solitude and contemplation proposes by itself an experimental monastic search. The daily routines of a community are no longer present and therefore the personal arrangement of the day and the prayer life of a hermit depend on a personal order and responsibility as well as on the movements of the Spirit. If one adds the search for dialogue and a common journey with people of other faiths, the life of a hermit is unique and a new experience every day. In the next chapter I offer some personal reflections on the organization of space, time, prayer, texts and symbolic objects within a hermitage, taking into account my own construction of an eremitic landscape.

Chapter 2

ORDERING TIME, SPACE AND MEDITATION TOGETHER

This chapter outlines the enormous possibilities of becoming a hermit, and a hermit that dwells on the oneness of the world religions. For in the case of cenobitic communities the eremitic road ahead is marked by a continuity in space with an abbey, a priory or a monastery. The community informs the hermit's life through a tradition in which there are innovations within the sacredness and tranquillity of things having been done previously. For example, and as outlined in the previous chapter, Thomas Merton became a hermit within the bounded lands of the Abbey of Gethsemani, thus having to organize his time but relying heavily on a monastic space already in existence. He could join the community for the Eucharist at times, or take his meal at the refectory if visitors arrived, and receive mail and seek help if he needed it.[1] However, in the case of the Hindu *sanyasi* and the Christian hermits without a monastic community, not only has time to be regulated but space should be recreated within a building, a tent or a caravan, by taking decisions on how space should reflect a way of life, the way of a hermit.[2]

EREMITICAL UNBOUNDED SPACES

The three realities of a challenging eremitic life, that is time, space and meditation, go together, because a hermit is not made by a property or a landscape, neither is time ordered because of the times in which a community comes together, nor do meditation and contemplation depend on a communal time or space, or even a hermitage. However, the harmony of these three categories can provide the necessary conditions in which the life of a hermit can happen. The freedom of a full invention of a cognitive reality never exists and the unbounded spaces are mediated by bounded spaces. Even the amplitude and platitude of the sands of the desert require a connection between the open space and the bounded possibilities of meeting the Absolute. For it is this act of love, what Charles de Foucauld called 'intercourse' between the hermit and the Absolute, that matters. Within that ongoing intercourse there is the clarity of purpose: to pray and to meditate takes most of the day, and other activities such as study or cooking or gardening are secondary. Indeed, I return to the sound and holy advice given to Abhishiktananda by his friend, the *sadhu* Harilal: 'There is only one book, the "living" book that is within you… Instead of reading, think (i.e. meditate); instead of thinking, keep essential silence within, a silence beyond… both the thought and the non-thought that within you meet the Supreme.'[3]

Otherwise the flow of love for God could become a dream, particularly if many guests and visitors take over the life of a hermitage. One well-meaning friend asked me if I directed meditation classes at the hermitage and I could only utter shy words in a soft voice: 'I don't. I just pray. You will be very welcome to come and pray if you want.' Another well-meaning scholar who heard that I was a hermit asked me if a group of hermits met frequently. My answer, once again quite apologetic, was that hermits do not usually meet; they like solitude not for the sake of solitude or loneliness but they like to spend time with the Absolute. And in order to spend time with the Absolute, one has to forget all the possible usefulness of one's place and all the characteristics of a community contribution in order to be just a hermit.

My hermitage, Arunachala Hermitage, evolved from being my studio to being a hermitage by natural causes. It is in the fishing village of Anstruther on the east coast of Scotland, in a series of villages where the first hermits of Scotland lived. Those hermits lived in a cave to meet the Absolute, to attain personal holiness and to share the poverty and renunciation of Jesus of Nazareth. Arunachala Hermitage is the ground floor of a larger building filled with small studios in the historic part of the town. It has one room, one bathroom and one kitchen. The name Arunachala, with all respect to Hindus, evokes the fact that the hermitage is a place where prayers and meditation mark a common journey between Christians, Buddhists and Hindus. For the Arunachala caves in India are sacred to Hindus, and it was there that Abhishiktananda had the first experiences of solitude, silence and renunciation. I wanted to express a total renunciation towards this common journey by choosing a name associated with Hinduism rather than Christianity, though I realize that a more traditional name would have been Holy Trinity or the Hermitage of Our Lady. I have been very much inspired by the experience that Abhishiktananda had at Arunachala, and I have spent several nights visualizing such experiences in which the togetherness of a Christian monk inside one cave contrasted with the solitude of a *sadhu* in another cave. For I have dwelt on a conversation that Abhishiktananda had with a *sadhu* named Harilal when he stayed at Arunachala in 1954, a conversation that he narrated to a friend in Paris. Thus, Abhishiktananda became friendly with Harilal the *advāitin*, who looked for him and 'tried to persuade him to take the final plunge into pure *advāita* and abandon every kind of religious observance'.[4] Abhishiktananda could not accept this proposal. After dwelling on this incident, and in a different era, it is plausible to suggest that a hermitage could develop its own rhythm of daily life only if it is not attached to or part of a monastery.

I have a second hermitage, Nalanda, in Santiago, Chile, as part of the Fundación Milarepa para el Diálogo con Asia, where I have started to provide space and opportunities for interfaith and intercultural dialogue. Nalanda has a different character, simply because it is located within a block of apartments in the centre of the city in the tradition of Carlo Carretto's *The Desert in the City*.[5] It is surrounded by people, cars and noise on purpose, because the silence of Nalanda recalls and actualizes the place of learning that Hindus and Buddhists had in India. The study of texts and the renunciation of noise causes the mind to explore areas of the conscious and the subconscious in silence, regardless if one is beside the sea, as in Scotland, or surrounded by students and civil servants, as in Chile.

Thus, once the wish to be a hermit occurs, the surroundings and the objects that fill a space start appearing, not the other way around. It is the search for the Absolute and the search for silence, contemplation and meditation that provides the foundation for the structural rest. One of the great challenges of space is to allow space to serve the hermit rather than vice versa. For the *kutiya* of Abhishiktananda was nothing more than a very light structure which allowed him to contemplate, to study, to do some cooking and to remain physically immersed in a space beside the Ganga, where he wanted to be. It is within such space that the challenges and creative moments of silence start solving the great challenge that a hermit faces: the tension between moments in which as a Christian one fills one's heart with God and Hindu and Buddhist perceptions of emptiness and nothingness. For the space designated as a hermitage would eventually reflect a spiritual path, and the objects that would fill the room would shout aloud the secrets of the hermit to others.

SACRED FLOORS AND SACRED RENUNCIATION

The first reality of my hermitage is the floor, the ground, the carpet. For I have chosen not to base prayer moments or sleeping moments in the fabulous world of furniture but on the realities of the floor. It is on the floor that I awake in the morning, and I prostrate myself with my forehead on the ground as a sign of adoration towards the Lord and personal submission and renunciation to anything that could render this path only a plausibility. I sleep on the floor, and I pray on the floor, because it is the floor that is common to all human beings and indeed to all sentient beings. The poor and the monks spend their lives sitting on the floor, and this is also the custom of Hindus and Buddhists who very easily accommodate themselves on the ground to pray, to eat and to sleep. Thus, the centrality of the floor of the only room I have within the hermitage.

I have followed the path of those monks such as Abhishiktananda, who found that the Christian monastic ways were enriched by a way of Hinduism, namely *Advāita Vedānta*, and a way of compassion and meditation in Buddhism, the Way of the Bodhisattva. Thus, *Advāita Vedānta* becomes not a concept to understand reality but a way to sustain the journey, a common journey with others. *Vedānta* literally means 'the end of the Vedas', and the end of the Vedas are the Upanishads.[6] Thus, *Vedānta* is the interpretation of the Upanishads (*sruti* or what has been heard) within their summarizing in the Brahma-Sūtras. Other sources include the Bhagavad Gitā, because the Gitā, together with the Rāmāyana and the Mahābhārata and Purānas, is assumed as a traditional central text with some authority (*smrti* or what has been remembered). The 'remembered' has the function to corroborate the 'heard'. Within *Vedānta* there are three traditions of thought, one of which is *Advāita Vedānta*. Thus *Advāita Vedānta*, according to Bartley, is 'a metaphysical monism saying that fundamental reality is featureless and tranquil consciousness'.[7] The other *Vedānta* suggest the unity of a complex reality (*Visistādvaita Vedānta*) and a strict monotheism with a realistic metaphysical pluralism (*Dvaita Vedānta*). For these three schools the *sruti* are the sole means of knowing (*pramāna*) what is beyond the senses and its interactions. The Upanishads then provide the knowledge about being (*brahman*), the soul (*ātman*), their common relation, the origin of the universe (from *brahman*), the consequences of action (*karma*) and the liberation from rebirth (*mokhta, mukti*). Thus, reason is only used in support of sacred texts because, after all, reasoning can bring further explanations and therefore texts have the authority for the knowing.

The Upanishads, meaning 'sitting beside', were composed between 800 and 300 BCE. In their variety and their different schools of interpretation they are to be interpreted in their totality and within the Sāmkhya theory of *satkāryavāda*: effects emanate from causes, and they do not differ substantially from them. Thus the nexus or parallelism of being (*analogia entis*) between the world and *brahman*, its cause. The Upanishads express the sense of sitting beside a master as a disciple, or making connections between different realities or placing one thing next to the other.[8] They arose within the transformations and the economic exchanges that took place in the kingdoms of the eastern Ganges with all trading roads leading to Kashi. Indeed, Wendy Doniger has argued that the idea of *karma* (action/merit) and its ways of operating reflect notions of trading and the exchange of goods so that *karma* 'can be accumulated, occasionally transferred, and eventually cashed in'.[9] Within the Upanishads, words from the Vedas take new meanings and new movements appear. Such newness creates a continuity from action and the divine fire that becomes in the case of *karma* merit as well as action, and in the case of *tapas* an ascetically generated inner heat as well as the heat of sacrificial action.

The Upanishads provided new layers within Hinduism that also provided new concepts for the possibility of an ascetic life and of renunciation. Thus, for example, the early *dharma-sutras* (ca. 300–100 BCE) mentioned four *ashramas* or ways of life that could be undertaken within a person's life: the chaste student (*brahmacharin*), the householder or family man (*grihastha*), the forest dweller (*vanaprastha*) and the renouncer (*sannayasin*). Previously these four were single options for life, but the theology of the *sannayasin* became a possibility to be combined with the forest dwellers. As a result, and by the second century CE, the four ways of life could be undertaken as stages of progression within life and therefore at any moment during a lifetime.

Within the Upanishads the individual self (soul, *atman*) and the universal Self (*brahman*) become one. Thus, the world of *brahman* is of monism, assuming that all living things are elements of a single, universal being. The result is an understanding of pantheism by which God is everything and everything is God. In the helpful summary by Wendy Doniger:

> This philosophy views the very substance of the universe as divine, and views that substance and that divinity as unitary. The pluralistic world has a secondary, illusory status in comparison with the enduring, real status of the underlying monistic being.[10]

To understand the construction or making of a hermitage, it is important to understand the utopic movement that all the world religions including Hinduism and Buddhism had, from trading centres and urban centres to the wilderness of caves, trees and forests. Thus, together with the Upanishads, the Aranyakas (the jungle books) expressed the philosophical investigations and meditations of those who fled back to the jungles at times when the trading centres, urban centres and kings and lords brought to them war, pestilence and slavery. Master and student sat under a tree in a setting that later was to be that of a monastery and a university; texts recording their conversations arose as part of human reflections within and outwith Hinduism. For example, the Brihadanranyaka ('Great Jungle Book') is an early Upanishad and the final section of the Shatapatha Brahmana, written, as most of the early Upanishads, in prose.[11]

Advāita Vedānta arose out of several authors and thinkers, mainly Samkara and Mandara Misra around 700 CE.[12] Both of them could be considered the founding fathers of *Advāita Vedānta*. Samkara produced commentaries on the Brahma-Sūtras, the Bhagavad Gita and the Upanishads, as well as the Upadesa-Sāhasri ('thousand teachings'). Samkara has the vision of a radical renouncer that questions the orthodox parameters of the mere existence of individual thinkers, agents and acts.[13] He elaborates originally on previous thinkers such as Gaudapāda (450–500 CE) who wrote the Agama-sāstra on the Mandukya Upanishad. Normal experience for him is no different than dreaming, because in both experiences only consciousness remains constant. It is the Supreme Soul that imagines itself in *bhāva* (individual entities) rather than vice versa. His contemporary Barthrhari spoke about the *sabda-advāita* understood as the 'non-dualism of meaning'. Within this process the *brahman* appears and manifests itself in many words, sounds and meanings that in the end are universal and an expression of a unitary mode of consciousness. For Barthrhari, words are identical and the objects that we see are manifestations of identical words but with diverse meanings.

Advāita is non-dualism or monism, and reality is only of one kind. Thus, according to the doctrine of *Advāita*, the *brahman* is an unconditional reality and the coincidence of being, consciousness and bliss. It is the realization of being and consciousness that ends ignorance and provokes the fulfilment of non-duality. In order to do so, the renouncers, the *advāitins*, renounce the possibility that extroverted forms of religion could bring the non-duality required in order to be one with the *brahman*. Being and consciousness become one by realization rather than by actions. This is a break with the Vedic rituals that through a priesthood and through communal rituals mediated human life and the absolute reality of *brahman*. Through meditation, thoughts and feelings disappear and the objective is no more than a meditative stage, without objective, in which being and consciousness become one. This meditative state is subversive and radical towards religious systems and ritual parameters of understanding a path, and certainly challenged not only orthodox Brahmanism but also the belief that life is *samsara* and the acquisition of *karma*. Because of this non-duality and the immateriality of the path, *advaita* also challenges the caste system, because it does hold that a particularly differentiated order could lead to the bliss of being and consciousness together.

It is within *Advaita Vedānta* and the world of the Upanishads that Abhishiktananda and the other Christian monks who pioneered a Christian–Hindu dialogue by action and renunciation found a home. There were reasons of monastic similarities such as contemplation, silence, fasting and studying. The central reason was the similarity of silence and an ascetic life in which they could find the monastic rhythm that they knew so well. However, within a Hindu conception of the lack of canon and an enormous variety of religious experience, Abhishiktananda and the others found it reassuring that within *Vedānta* there were central texts, the Upanishads, that were considered somehow important and inspired.

It was within *advaita* as non-duality that Abhishiktananda felt the tension between his notion of the Christ as a European and his wish to worship with a Christ dressed in Indian clothing, and he felt the mark that Hindus were making in him when he wrote:

> A hidden spiritual sympathy, this sense of the Unity, of the ONE, of God at the source of my being, of the fading out of this 'ego' as soon as you penetrate into the interior of yourself so as to reach the unique 'I'.[14]

This tension had already been felt before his stay at the Arunachala caves. After his stay and in his spiritual diary he wrote: 'Plunge into oneself, at one's own greatest depth. Forget my own *aham*, be lost in the *aham* of the divine *Atman* which is at the source of my being, of my awareness of being.'[15] During his second stay at Arunachala, one of the visitors to the Ramana Ashram, a *sadhu* called 'Harilal' by Abhishiktananda, 'tried to convince him to abandon every kind of religious observance, something that Abhishiktananda was not prepared to do'.[16] However, Abhishiktananda admitted that it was during Lent in 1953 and at the Arunachala cave of Aruptal Tirtham that he understood *advāita*.[17] On returning to Shantivanam Ashram he always felt that he had been happier at the Arunachala caves. Back in the ashram and trying to practise a non-duality, he wrote about his duties as a guest master: 'it distracts me from my "advaitic"…life at Arunachala, with all that this gives of peace and depth, and at the same time of anguish for the Christian'.[18]

I empathize with these choices and, while I entered Hinduism like Abhishiktananda with a curiosity about the public Vedic rituals of fire and the sacredness of rivers and mountains, I found it comforting to have the freedom to listen to the silence in a hermitage and to read, study and carry with me at all times a version of the Upanishads as texts that embrace the Vedantic ideal of unity in diversity. Thus, within my choice of *Advāita Vedānta* as an exploration into the fullness of Christ in daily life, my hermitage does not need all the objects, musical instruments and furniture required by Christian monasteries, Hindu Vedic temples or Buddhist monasteries. Apart from the floor, a small stool or table is required for the celebration of the Eucharist, and a library and a desk help in the study of the Gospels, the Upanishads and *The Way of the Bodhisattva*. In the reading of texts, in the form of *lectio divina*, understood as slowly undertaking the connection with the text through particular words and sentences, there is the possibility of expanding the inclusiveness of a non-duality into a non-sectarian existence.[19] Thus, the lessons of *Advāita Vedānta* bring the possibility and necessity of the non-contradiction and the inclusiveness of all theistic and non-theistic traditions, particularly of Hinduism and Buddhism – non-theistic traditions that historically were closely connected and that today continue informing Christian interfaith dialogue.

THE WALLS OF CONTEMPLATION AND TANKAS

For years after the birth of the Lord Buddha, Hinduism and Buddhism lived side by side under the patronage of local kings. Those patrons did not feel the need to distinguish different rights for Hindus or Buddhists or to distinguish different rites. Some of the insistence on vegetarianism in Hinduism came from the respect of all sentient beings in Buddhism as well as the doctrine of non-violence (*ahimsa*) that Hinduism and Buddhism acquired from Jainism. Hinduism tried to include Buddhism within the many varieties of Hinduism by making the Buddha one of the incarnations of Vishnu. It was only later, with the Muslim conquest and the end of the Buddhist universities, particularly Nalanda, that Hinduism and Buddhism became quite differentiated within and without India.

Within Arunachala Hermitage the ground has become the point of union of a common humanity and the floor of meditation and enlightenment. However, the main wall by chance became a visual reminder of the presence of the healing Buddha and of Tibet within the hermitage. During June 2014, a group of us attended a special *puja* at the Geden Choeling Nunnery in McLeod Ganj above Dharamsala. During lunch with the abbot and a nun who knew English, we discussed the possibility of helping them to continue their education programme. After all, Geden Choeling was one of the few nunneries in which doctorates in Buddhism had been pursued by nuns. On the evening before the day that we were leaving Dharamsala for Delhi, two nuns came with a majestic *tanka* that we were told we should bring to Scotland to protect us. It was sent by Abbot Kampo and became the seal of the Tibetan Buddhist presence within the hermitage. The *tanka* has the image of the healing Buddha and the standards of the Geluk, the order of the Dalai Lamas. Healing is something that can abound when prayers are said, and good energies are sent to all those who ask for them. I prostrate, praying for those who have asked for prayers and those whom I see suffering through the news. This is the most important effect that a hermitage can have. It is no more than a room within a landscape which offers space for silence and meditation, for prayers and for salutations in order to alleviate the suffering of others and to accompany pilgrims and the poor and the marginalized in a common journey.

POVERTY, POWER AND PROSPERITY

Historically and in the context of Asia and Egypt, hermitages were rocks and caves within social contexts of survival and danger. Hermits had very little to eat and drink and only one habit, because most people around them had very little as well. The rise of monastic prosperity through hard work meant that hermits attached to an abbey had their meals either delivered or served in the refectory and that they could have heat, electricity and whatever comforts they needed. This was the case of Thomas Merton, who cooked in a stove, had a record player and a typewriter, and could bring his laundry to the abbey if necessary. One recalls the great disappointment of Bede Griffiths at the establishment of Fr Mahieu's monastery, Kurisumala, in Kerala, when, instead of establishing an ashram, Mahieu's dream as a Cistercian started to be realized with the arrival of cattle, not only to sustain the needs of the monastery but as part of a regional programme of agricultural development. The ideal of the Hindu *sanyasi*, and therefore of the Christian *sanyasi*, clashed with that of self-reliance in that the reliance was on God's providence through alms and donations of food, something quite natural for those who have taken the saffron robes in the Indian context. In my own experience, I remembered the impression it made on me when I lived in London at a religious house, where Fr Walter Boyle SVD and Fr Thomas Lynch SVD, two of the priests who were leading the seminary formation of young seminarians, lived very simple lives and didn't use a bed but slept on the floor covered with blankets. Both had lived in India.

It is a fact that hermitages in the northern hemisphere do not necessarily share the hardships of hermits who live in the Himalayas or in Asia in general. Therefore, within the creation of a hermitage, issues that I would include within the concepts of poverty, power and prosperity need to be considered at the start of a hermitage and within ongoing reflections on its very existence. The hermit follows the life of the Master, who did not have a home but was an itinerant preacher, centred on a life of prayer with his Father. In the context of an interfaith hermitage, the hermit is somebody who uses Buddhist and Hindu practices to respond to a calling to sit in a cell and wait for God. In all these practices, reflections related to a style of life that tries to be as close to renunciation, detachment and poverty as possible cannot be ignored. Liberation, be it from other activities, from the senses or from the mind, is only meaningful if it leads to a closeness with God and brings peace, liberation and bliss to others. For the Christian Bodhisattva does not measure levels of comfort, conformity or usefulness but has renounced the possibilities of being comforted to sit with God and find bliss in the Absolute.

The ethical responsibility of being a hermit connects directly with the foundations of the Christian faith and the two central commandments: to love God and to love thy neighbour. In prayer, meditation and renunciation the hermit loves God and loves their neighbour through prayer and silence. As in the case of Buddhism and Hinduism, the hermit renounces the distractions of noise and futile worries to help other human beings and sentient beings on their journey. The hermit journeys together with them, and in doing so learns from them and is transformed by them. In my work on Christian–Buddhist dialogue I have related the terms and implications of 'liberation' within Tibetan Buddhism and Latin American liberation theology.[20] I argued that 'it is the realization of suffering that assigns a central tenet of love and compassion to both Christianity and Buddhism', so that 'liberation comes from detachment from riches in Christianity, from detachment from a material world that is an illusion in Buddhism'.[21] I extend these preoccupations for poverty and riches within a life of interfaith dialogue with Hinduism, because the ethical responsibility of material renunciation comes not only through a monastic renunciation but also through a solidarity with other human beings who are poor and marginalized, particularly women and those outside the caste system in India.[22]

For the poor as a different social category exists only as far as our ill-conceived religious identity, our self-proclaimed purity and our self-esteemed holiness and religious status is put forward. Otherwise we are one with the poor and with all other faiths and non-faiths, because we are all human beings on a journey with different occupations and fates. Thus, the 14th Dalai Lama in his 1989 Nobel Prize Lecture opened the occasion with the following remark:

> I am always reminded that we are all basically alike: we are all human beings. Maybe we have different clothes, our skin is of a different colour, or we speak different languages. This is on the surface. But basically, we are the same human beings. That is what binds us to each other.[23]

I want to return to Latin America, as I did in my Christian–Buddhist dialogue, knowing that Buddhism and Hinduism have been intrinsically connected since the time of the Lord Buddha and the working together that took place at Nalanda University centuries ago. For, it is symptomatic of an age of globalization that the contextual and the localized have provided more and more a link between human beings. Thus, liberation theology starting in Latin America provided points of encounter with Africa and Asia, and theologians such as Jon Sobrino SJ developed further theological cooperation and experiences by experiencing other contexts. Thus Sobrino's work on a Latin American Christology became more universal after the assassination of his friend Ignacio Ellacuría SJ in El Salvador. Sobrino, as a member of the Jesuit community of the Central American University in El Salvador, would have also been shot by the Salvadorian soldiers who assassinated the Jesuit community at the university had he not been away in Thailand attending conferences. One could say that he was saved by Asia to witness to the truth of the poor. And so he did, in an ongoing dialogue with Ellacuría.

Sobrino rephrased the dictum by Origen and Cyprian as *extra ecclesiam nulla salus* into *extra pauperes nulla salus* – outside the poor there is no salvation.[24] He noted that after Vatican II Schillebeeckx had also paraphrased the patristic sentence by enunciating *extra mundum nulla salus* – outside the world there is no salvation.[25] The possibility of hope and redemption from power and prosperity has not been a trait of liberation within the Catholic Church, while lately it has appeared as an influence from some evangelical quarters, particularly in Africa and Latin America. However, the poverty of Jesus of Nazareth, who made the choice to be born in a province outside Jerusalem, who went with his parents into exile and who surrounded himself with those dispossessed and rejected by the society of his time, speaks clearly of a divine preferential option for the dispossessed (a preferential option for the poor). As it was in Latin America after Vatican II, the poor were the ones who listened to the gospel of hope, equality and justice and educated the clergy and the religious in the ways of the Lord, beginning with Monsignor Romero of El Salvador.

It is through the lessons of the poor that a hermit must see its Christian renunciation of riches, power and prestige. It is through this renunciation and simple style of life that the Christian hermit can be in communion with the Hindu renouncers and the Buddhist monks. A simple room (with no bed), a toilet and a kitchen is already a luxury for many in Asia. However, dining tables and chairs are a luxury that can only be found in the homes of teachers, merchants and civil servants in India. Thus, a reminder of an ethical life in solidarity with the poor and the marginalized becomes part of a process of Christian renunciation. I have been asked many times if I can or I can't do something. My response is that one continues a journey with the Lord and divine, and personal demands follow processes of inner conversion and outer solidarity with others. Vegetarianism comes into this discussion. Not every Hindu or Buddhist is a vegetarian, but vegetarianism expresses respect for sentient beings on the one hand and solidarity with those who can't afford meat on the other. Renunciation expresses solidarity with others, and certainly with the poor and the marginalized affected in the past by a colonial Christianity, as well as those Hindus affected by the caste system in India.

THE SPACE FOR MEDITATION AND ENCOUNTER

It is late on Sunday evening, and the evening prayer has already been said (see Appendix 3). Today there is nobody else in the hermitage, and the silence invites one to sit and connect with Hindu friends from India. The advent of the internet allows a hermit to use technology to join devout Hindus in Varanasi in their own prayers and after to pray for them. The daily gospel and a text of the Upanishads is read daily at Arunachala Hermitage (Scotland) and Nalanda Hermitage (Chile). Other faiths and fellow pilgrims are also present, because as soon as they heard that other faiths were present at prayer at this hermitage, they sent me a small statue or a sacred painting to represent them. I think particularly of a scholar in Japan who sent me a small statue of Jizō (地蔵), a bodhisattva of the Japanese Buddhist pantheon in order to be present at our prayers.[26] It is fitting to remember the wisdom of Shantideva:

> *And now as long as space endures,*
> *As long as there are beings to be found,*
> *May I continue likewise to remain*
> *To drive away the sorrows of the world.*[27]

In the following chapter I explore some of the conversations I have had with Hindus in India as well as in Scotland, and the visit by Hindus to Scotland and to Arunachala Hermitage.

Chapter 3

INTERFAITH ENCOUNTERS AND SILENCE

In the previous chapter, issues of space and time, of order and disorder within a hermitage and within dialogue, were explored. It is within these spaces and times that dialogue can take place when two strangers meet in trust to share their experience of God and the Absolute and their way of life.[1] This way of life that seems diverse becomes the constancy of the dialogue in which silence prevails, the silence of listening, first to a stranger, then to another human being and, finally, to a fellow pilgrim.[2] The first and foundational encounter, though, is that of two fellow human beings who share joys and sufferings, even when they are not aware of such a journey together.[3]

Thus it was that during 2015 and 2016 I shared the privilege of silence and dialogue with Kabir Babu, a scholar of Hinduism and researcher, through many conversations, several meals and a common purpose: to listen to the Absolute through the dialogue of our own existences, one Hindu, the other Christian. Our conversations developed into other conversations of the unexpected – an unexpected journey in which differences were sharpened and commonalities became a daily occurrence. Those surprises continued with a change of location and environment. The initial conversations took place in St Andrews amid Christian theologians, where Kabir Babu encountered a place to reflect on his beliefs and thoughts even when surrounded by European Christian theologians and scholars. In June 2016 he hosted me and my life companion at Amritsar during our visit to India within my annual visit to the Tibetan enclave at Dharamsala. Conversations took place at his home, at the Cascade Centre for Education in Amritsar, during our visit to Guru Nanak Dev University where he previously studied, and during a long journey by car from Amritsar to Dharamsala.[4]

The following transcriptions and inscriptions of common realities and diverse understandings of being Christian and Hindu confirmed the possibility of firmly believing that in fact interfaith dialogue is possible.[5] However, interfaith dialogue takes place first at the level of a common humanity when strangers meet, and then such common humanity is developed at meetings or conferences. Those two people in dialogue have a history, they belong to a ritual way within Christianity or Hinduism, and their dialogue is not neutral or ethereal but is always mediated by daily events, family life and state of mind or consciousness, as well as emotions.

The first set of conversations took place in St Andrews, Scotland, from 2015 to 2016. Both of us were coming from somewhere else: Kabir from Amritsar (India) and myself from the Arunachala Hermitage in Anstruther, Scotland. Some conversations also took place in virtual reality. A second set of conversations took place in Amritsar during June 2016 in the presence of other pilgrims and under the protection of the Sri Harmandir Amritsar. The third set of conversations took place in the context of the conference that followed the signing of the St Andrews Declaration for a Shared Humanity (23–25 September 2016) in St Andrews, Scotland, where a common silence was experienced, particularly on Sunday 25 September. During that day and coinciding with the last day of the St Andrews Conference, the Hindus Ramesh and Kabir Babu joined an interfaith meditation in silence and took part in the morning

Christian service at the University of St Andrews Chapel. After the chapel service and at the St Andrews Pier, Kabir Babu led people of other faiths on the changing of the OM and visited Arunachala Hermitage in Anstruther during the afternoon where the three of us, Kabir, Ramesh and me, visited the hermitage and had conversations at the Pier before having some afternoon tea.

THE FIRST ENCOUNTER: ST ANDREWS

Let's start with the first encounters of two pilgrims who do not know very much about each other and sit together trying to find a common ground through the Upanishads.

KABIR BABU

I was born into a Hindu family. My introduction to Hindu religiosity was subtle and organic. I have a faint recollection of my earliest childhood wherein most of my afternoons were spent with my grandmother in front of the home shrine with an assortment of deities on display (for offering prayers). I used to chant the Gayatri Mantra every morning upon insistence from my mother, as she felt it would make my life more prosperous. I was a mischievous child and was often in some kind of trouble due to my adventures. As a result, my mother would offer prayers in my name to Surya Devta (the Sun God). So it could be said that, even though religion was all around me, I never felt indoctrinated, even in retrospect. Socially, on the other hand, faith was never an option – it was an assumption for the most part. Be it the Puranic trinity of Bramah Vishnu Mahesh or the cult of Krishna and Rama (who were Avatars of Vishnu); as a Hindu you either believed in one of them/all of them/some of them (depending on your lineage) and their abilities to impact your spiritual as well as material life, or you adopted other smaller cults like Hanuman, Ganesha, Goddess Durga, Goddess Kali, etc. The list is virtually endless; as I mention above, 'an assortment of deities'.

In the caste hierarchy I was born as a Brahmin (being a Kashmiri Pundit), thereby providing me with the highest caste status. Having lived my entire life amongst the urban population of North India, I never quite experienced caste as a social evil. Probably because belonging to the top of the social hierarchy brings with it an inherent sense of ignorance toward the lower castes. The socioeconomic segregation is such that I (unknowingly) never had any friends from the lowest castes until the age of 14. Due to the nature of my parents' job and their predisposition toward a nomadic lifestyle, I travelled across the length and breadth of North India. So much so that by the age of 18 I had lived in four cities and attended ten schools. I studied in secular private schools, Sikh missionary schools as well as Hindu Arya Samaji schools. My experience with these schools, a general bent towards the liberal arts and my father's socialist upbringing led to an outcome that, much to the dismay of my mother as well as my grandmother, was quite contrary to the general religious milieu. I became a hardcore atheist. I discovered Marxism and often found myself immersed in Marxist literature. I believed it was hard to be a capitalist in a country as poor as India.

During my undergrad studies in social sciences and while experimenting with Marxist ideology, I started questioning traditional approaches towards social interaction between the 'devotee' and his/her 'faith' in India, analysing the 'God–Men' business in my term-paper titled 'Rational Gods: Understanding Religion through Economics'. I argued that in the 'religious marketplace' of India the commodification of religion and religiosity is such that salvation is a product, preachers are capitalists and devotees are consumers who make rational decisions with 'faith investments'. My utilitarian view of religion was too radical for my surroundings, and to further this understanding I came to the UK to pursue further studies and further research.

In the midst of Western society, away from my family for the first time, I began to unravel the problems through my own approach. In this respect, a distinct numinous experience at Durham Cathedral on the 'Remembrance Sunday' evening of 2013 stood out. As people shared stories of loss, coupled with the novelty of the situation and Mozart's *Requiem* playing in the background, I felt something that I have never since been able to recreate. I was propelled towards the realization that in my theory I had not accounted for the spiritual aspects of religion. I wrote the following poem on that day:

WHERE I AM FROM

I am from the echoes of the past, from the yearnings of
the future and the slipping stillness of the present.
From the millions of moments that are lost, from
the millions that are still to be and from the
few that are staring at me fearful of loss.
I am from my father's reality, from my son's
dreams and from my own expectations.
I am from the vanquished ideas, from the renaissance of
the vanquished and the decadence of the revived.
I am from the redemption of truth. I am its only true enemy,
its only true companion and its only true witness.
I am from nothingness from the absolute emptiness, from the
place where it all began, where it all shall end and where
from it shall all loop again, to bring me to you who see
me for what I am, walk with me without asking…
WHERE I AM FROM.[6]

That year in Durham was a harsh experience, considering the cultural shock, the absolute solitude and dearth of resources. I would not go as far as to say that I found religion that year, but I did make room for the possibility of spiritual experiences. Furthermore, the encounter with my sociology and anthropology of religion professor (Professor Douglas James Davies) introduced me to authors like Roy Rappaport, Mircea Eliade, Victor Turner, Eric Wolf, W. Stanner and Susan Harding, among others. As my education became globalized, I found my expression becoming more localized. During this period, I worked on the concept of over-sanctification in Hinduism, the religio-political scenario in the Indian Kashmir, identity changes within Sikhism and the theory and practice of *karma* in Hindu philosophy.

I started interacting with the philosophy of Hinduism, as I came to the understanding that there were merits to religion but its structural integrity had been compromised with respect to its interactions in the social, political and economic sphere throughout history. For some reason, even though I never identified myself as a Hindu (in the conventional sense of the word), I started to peel off the layers of Hinduism and developed a more rounded understanding of its institutions, their philosophical backgrounds, their spiritual merits and their social demerits. I eventually arrived upon caste in Hinduism, as it is probably one of the most repressive religious institutions deeply embedded in the social psyche of an average Hindu as well as intertwined within the social fabric of Indian consciousness.

Hinduism is one of the oldest faiths in the world. Its history is one that to this day remains a matter of debate and deliberation, due to the lack of historical accounts and archaeological evidence. However, the sources informing scholars of the 'Hindu way of life' have been under great scrutiny due to the multitude of interpretations they have to offer. This, in turn, has led to a considerably large amount of scholarship being produced which diverges one from another on the most basic issues. Caste is only one such issue among many others. To understand and make intelligible observations on the subject, I have used Roy Rappaport as an essential tool when I revisit the earliest history of Hinduism in my research. Durkheim states in the *Elementary Forms of Religious Life* that there is no religion that is not both a cosmology and a speculation about the divine. It brought me to a premature deduction that religion is born out of the ability of the human mind to wonder.[7] This deduction, however premature, has informed my judgement on the subject of religion both consciously and subconsciously. Rappaport, who has been inspired by Durkheimian ideas among others, has taken it a step further in stating that religion is humanity's way of ascribing meaning to an otherwise meaningless universe.[8] However, the birth of religion, as it may be, is not the subject of my enquiry. This reference to the birth of religion is merely a modest attempt at providing a precursor to the discussion that shall follow. But my revisitation of the earliest period in Hinduism and possibly its birth is embedded in capturing this aforementioned 'ascription of meaning' by the earliest theologians to an admittedly meaningless universe. It is an attempt to capture the essence of Hindu philosophy and the theological background to the formation of caste. Many believe that caste cannot be done away with due to its deep-rooted integration with Hinduism. Also, caste as a Hindu institution is either denied or justified by most Hindu theologians. I believe that by focusing on the loss of sacredness and meaning in Hinduism due to the institution of caste as well as its historical perversion (hence a symbiotic theological perversion), it is possible to change the discourse on caste within Hindu theology.

This was an unexpected opening, as it brought to life the possibilities and the unknown surprises of two human beings who were strangers before the mystical language of poetry arose as the bridge between two ways of life, between the two constraints put by two different civilizations. My response was the following.

MARIO I. AGUILAR

It has been my intention, my wish and my desire to follow the ways of prayer, love of God and love of neighbour, that could locate me closer to Buddhists and Hindus. It is in their traditions, exemplified by the monastic orders of the Geluk and the *sadhus* of the 13 akharas, that I have found a deep resonance with the Camaldolese Benedictines, my religious family, a Catholic monastic order of hermits.[9] Within that resonance I have found the silence of God who sits beside me and smiles at the encounter. God does not speak to me but sits beside me on the ground as an eternal companion whom I respect, I treasure and I enjoy hours of silence with. It is in that dissonance of sound and silence, form and absence of form, contemplation and attrition that dialogue has taken place. Dialogue as the absence of ordinary utterances coming out of the mouth but utterances that have come out of the heart. Noisy moments of silence in which Christian and Hindu caves have been united in that symphony of a divine presence. Such presence has been expressed through the daily recitation of prayers and mantras, of divine chanting and the thanksgiving of devotees who chant the OM and the Eucharistic thanksgiving, together, in India, in Europe and at the shores of the ocean in Scotland.

I was raised in Chile, in South America, where a Catholic majority has had a very recent twentieth-century influence in the presence of Cistercians and Benedictines, and where I never met a Hindu or a Buddhist, or a Muslim. Those first encounters took place more than 30 years ago in London. I was shown the silence of prayer by Dom Bernard Orchard, a holy English Benedictine from Ealing Abbey in London. Later, in the summer of 1985, a South African Jesuit guided my 30 days' retreat, the Ignatian Exercises, at Loyola Hall, Liverpool. Between 1987 and 1988 I lived in the desert sands of northern Kenya, where Christians were only a handful and a Muslim Waso Boorana population responded to the daily calls to prayer and kept the month of Ramadan in between their hope and their camels.[10] It was there that my previous readings of Carlo Carretto guided me through my time in the desert with Muslim nomads, and under the stars I discovered that I was very happy with God and with human beings of other religions.[11]

I longed to combine the silence of prayer with the care of neighbours. The wisdom of a Jesuit who listened to me for several years in Edinburgh led me to the wonderful discovery that there was a religious family that was contemplative but allowed its members to live their daily life on their own as hermits with engagement with Buddhists and with the religious world of India (the Camaldolese Benedictines).[12] One of their members was Bede Griffiths.[13] And so it was that having arrived in Anstruther to a property of one room, one bathroom and a kitchen, I developed the space for a hermitage dedicated to pray with Buddhists and Hindus daily. The conversations with Kabir Babu, a scholar of Hinduism, developed in St Andrews during 2015–2016, were the confirmation that, within a world of diverse significance, God, the Father of all, can be reached and understood more fully by being mindful of a common journey with other human beings, particularly those that follow the traditions of Hinduism and Buddhism.

I have described in a previous chapter the possibilities of creating a landscape and a location where traditions can encounter each other and where the visualization of Buddhism and the fire awareness of Hinduism can bring a togetherness with others in the name of God. A hermit and a sinner, I have experienced great consolation and affirmation by the example of those Christian monks who lived in India among Hindus and by Hindus and Buddhists who have taught me like a child their way of a spiritual journey. In particular, Geshe Lakhdor of Dharamsala and His Holiness the 14th Dalai Lama have been kind and strict examples of a deep self-awareness in meditation and prayer and a close connection to human beings that we encounter in our daily life. It is at Arunachala Hermitage (Anstruther) that monks and deities have sat in silence, on the floor, triggering in me a deep warmth of the encounter and a loud dialogue in silence. I can recall the first encounter with a young Tibetan student in Dharamsala, in June 2014, far away from his parents who lived in Nepal, and who remained in utter silence sitting beside me after having visited a Tibetan temple. Looking at the high peaks and the snow and both of us in silence, we remained united for a lifetime sitting on a bench expressing our hopes for the future without a word. Dialogue is the silence of the journey that takes place every day in the awareness of our togetherness without a rational understanding of the moment. However, this dialogue continues with the joys of discovering each other's traditions, forms, likes and dislikes, without the possibility of destroying God's symphony of silence and dialogue.

After this exchange of our fundamental histories and ways of dialogue, further conversations with Kabir relating to texts and contexts followed weekly. Sometimes these conversations were shorter but they usually lasted two to three hours. During the conversations time disappeared, silence was present and the realization of a mystical togetherness opened the possibility of a visit to Kabir's home in Amritsar. However, with the start of the interfaith year at the Centre for the Study of Religion and Politics (CSRP) at the University of St Andrews, a centre which I founded and have directed for 11 years, our conversations shifted from our symbolic present to the meetings that were to take place in India during June 2016 to prepare for a return visit of more than one Hindu from Amritsar to St Andrews. After my visit to Amritsar a return visit from Amritsar would provide further opportunities for dialogue in the context of the signing of the St Andrews Declaration on a Shared Humanity (see Appendix 6).

THE SECOND ENCOUNTER: AMRITSAR

During June 2016 Kabir Babu and myself met once again in Amritsar, where he was staying with his parents and extended family. My life companion and I had visited Delhi to discuss with the Ambassador of Chile, Mr Andrés Barbé González, the possibilities of his support for future interfaith dialogue in Delhi. Being the ambassador of a non-theistic persuasion, we had a frank exchange on religious issues, and I proposed to him that he could facilitate some of the proceedings planned for the signing of the India Declaration in June 2017 (see Appendix 6). I realized that the ambassador was exercising caution on issues of interfaith, a somewhat delicate subject in India not only after India's independence and partition but also in the current climate of more strained relations between the government of India and non-Hindu religious organizations.[14]

Further dialogue took place with a young man who was working at one of the Delhi hotels and who remained single because of work in Delhi. It was clear that discussions on Shiva and the powerful culinary effects on dialogue of a Murg curry developed my sense that the journey to the Punjab would be auspicious and that the conversations with Kabir Babu had paved a deep sense of a human commonality that I had not experienced in my previous journeys into India.

One of the central tenets of interfaith dialogue is respect for the other and the acquisition of knowledge, experiential and textual, about somebody else's tradition. Thus, my life companion and I proceeded with a young guide to visit the Sri Harimandir Sahib, the Golden Temple. It was midday, and it was extremely hot in the Holy City of the Sikhs. Without shoes and with heads covered as expected, we entered the temple's compound and proceeded with hundreds of pilgrims through the avenues that surround the inner waters of the temple, prostrating ourselves on the stones where saints were revered. The water we drank and the food we were given restored some of our energies, and the music that we shared with holy musicians gave joy to our heart. It seemed that we would have to be there for hours, days and years to share the lives of those who welcomed us. It was the music of divine silence and the reverence for the scriptures that were read that gave new energies to the pilgrimage and prepared us for a day of dialogue and communion with Kabir Babu, his family, his teachers and those who came to the conversation organized by the Cascade Centre for Education. The Sikhs' love for music was soothing within the heat of the day, and after three hours of pilgrimage we returned to our guest house in Amritsar to continue reading the soothing Sikh scriptures:

> O my Best Friend, O Divine Guru, please enlighten me with the Name of the Lord.
>
> Through the Guru's Teachings, the Naam is my breath of life. The Kirtan of the Lord's Praise is my life's occupation.[15]

It was in the early evening after the pilgrimage that I wrote the India Declaration for a Shared Humanity (see Appendix 6). In my pilgrim's fervour, I exalted the possibilities of a land in which temples, shrines, mosques, churches, sacred groves and sacred landscapes seem to overwhelm the spaces taken for the purposes of commerce, because in India the Greco-Roman division of life disappears and pilgrims can eat while they continue praying, and the constancy of prayer and chanting resounds in every shop and in every corner. Human activity is classified in caste and division, and social tensions exude religious discrimination and tension. However, once the pilgrim is on their way, there is a goodness that is socially recognized. Thus a foreigner like myself could be welcomed as a pilgrim and encouraged to pray many times, to remain at the Golden Temple, even, if I wanted, for the rest of my life.

On the following morning, my life companion and I visited Kabir Babu's home. The visit became an ongoing extended dialogue about life and about a journey, in which a Hindu family did not hesitate to express their views and their sense of life. We had the opportunity to discuss the ways in which religious traditions are accepted and lived by a family, and they do not necessarily have one or many traditions present in their lives but several traditions are lived at the same time. The essence of the diversity of Hinduism requires not only a constant conversation but the possibility that new elements and new members of the family could also bring challenges that need to be mediated through a common understanding and a variety of ways of dressing, eating and praying.

It was clear that what Kabir Babu had hinted in our conversations in St Andrews was ever present: before the religious classification over-stretched by the presence of the British colonial power and the partition of India, Hindus and Muslims lived together and respected a wide variety of ritual and non-theistic experiences. Within a Hindu and Muslim India, social practices and intermarriage do exist, and the very strong family tradition of home altars and home gods mediates the diversity within members of a biological and symbolic family.

I could describe the hours within the Babu household as an ongoing philosophical discussion mediated by different generations and consecrated with food eaten in common. Within such discussion answers and interventions were not made only in direct speech but also through poetry. Thus Kabir's sister read, aided by her phone, a poem that she had written for her parents. The poem had the Upanishadic sense of the circular belonging of the non-created in which her parents and her were in a constant circle of creation/non-creation, words/silence, and possibilities that were expressed through a silent cosmic existence that sometimes could not be expressed through a dialogue but through poetry.

The poem that Sunra Babu read is called 'From You to Me', and the text, written by Sunra Babu, reads as follows:

> *I am talking about the time,*
> *When sky first saw the earth,*
> *Holding to self and all eternity,*
> *When life was created in thought and conceived in vision,*
> *Where intimacy and sense of touch had*
>   *found new dimensions,*
> *And silence had a language of its own,*
> *When first, mind, soul and body, tranquillized movement*
> *And stillness bred motion,*

The aura of the ways my beginning
When dreams took shape of reality,
I am blessed by your togetherness,
My feet hold strong to two rocks beneath me,
With you two always above me,
You let me fly with time and in action,
You are my hope for the future, my faith in the past,
My present is your living
Canvasing my existence, you gave me identity,
And now stand, to move for you,
Holding both of you tight, clutching happiness and sorrow,
With my potential unchallenged.[16]

Sunra Babu wrote this poem in 2005, when she was 18 years old, for her parents' anniversary that year. When she was growing up, and even today to some extent, she saw herself as a combination of both her mother and father, a refined version in a new time, a product of both their worlds. Sunra's idea, expressed through the poem, was to express the wonder of the coming together that was her beginning, the idea of her being.[17]

The narrative of the poem, discussed on that day at the Babus' home in Amritsar, presupposed an inflection on the creativity of the non-created because there is no creator God in Hinduism as there is in Christianity. She thanked her parents for coming together within the forces of nature that create and recreate life every day, instead of thanking God as a personal Creator who looks after his people. For the Brahmanical teachings, based on the Vedas, have understood the first principle as immortal and outside time and space. 'Hindus believe that we are immortal by nature: one is essentially an indestructible soul or spirit that is contingently attached to an embodied life.'[18]

It is within such embodied life that India has provided a place where ancient civilizations provided philosophical explanations that allowed not theoretical discussions but the affirmation of knowledge as the way to exit the human wheel of life. If classical

Hinduism, the later developments of the Upanishads and the temple worship of many manifestations of *brahman* provided countless Hinduisms, Buddhism also started in India. Islam arrived from Arabia and, while violent clashes within feudal armies and religious narratives took place, in fact, they provided the establishment of Hinduism, Buddhism and Islam within India, followed by Jainism and Sikhism, making India a cosmopolitan milieu for human and divine ideas. The advent of the Raj provided the institutionalization of Christianity and the possibility for India to be the centre for religious strife and religious dialogue.

It is within such a historical context that the India Declaration for a Shared Humanity was discussed at the home of the Babus and minor changes made so as to arrive at the final text signed and read in Delhi in June 2017 (see Appendix 6). In the evening of that Sunday of June 2016 I gave a short lecture hosted by the Cascade Centre for Education at a Sikh community centre in Amritsar in the presence of Hindus and several Sikh members of staff of the Guru Nanak Dev University of Amritsar.

After a very fruitful discussion on a common humanity, issues of dialectical materialism, Marxism and the nature of religious studies, I was invited to visit the Guru Nanak Dev University on the following day as I was departing for Dharamsala. During the visit I gave a short lecture on a shared humanity and my host, Dr Balwant Singh Dhillon, explained the contribution of Sikhism to inter-religious dialogue, reminding me that the Shri Guru Granth Sahib, the Sikh scriptures, contained verses of the scriptures of other religions.[19] Thus, the founding guru, Shri Guru Nanak Dev Ji (1469–1538), argued that there is no Hindu and that there is no Muslim.[20] Thus, the Granth, compiled by Guru Gobind Singh, contains compositions by six gurus, namely Guru Nanak, Guru Angad, Guru Amar Das, Guru Ram Das, Guru Arjan and Guru Teg Bahadur.[21] The discussions on the need to get to know other traditions led to the invitation to continue these conversations, and I was shown some of the relics and objects that belonged to the Sikh founder. If I look back on this visit to the Sikh University, I recognize that I need to read the Sikh scriptures as a point of respect for the Sikhs and in order to try to understand better the Sikh way of life after my visit to the Golden Temple.

THE THIRD ENCOUNTER: ST ANDREWS AND ANSTRUTHER

After our encounter in Amritsar and my return to the UK, I started in earnest the preparations for the signing of the St Andrews Declaration for a Shared Humanity that took place in St Andrews, Scotland, on 23 September 2016; a signing that was followed by a conference on the theme and practice of silence in Christianity, Hinduism and Buddhism (see Appendix 6).

Kabir and Ramesh Babu signed the Declaration and took part in the proceedings that followed. Indeed, during the ceremony of the signing of the Declaration and after a formal introduction to the history and purpose of the Declaration, Kabir Babu chanted the OM – in this case, a privilege of those of Brahminic origin, like him. During the conference Kabir presented the paper 'Before It All Began: Silence and Purushasukta in Hinduism', which outlined the ongoing fresh understanding of silence and beginning, a theme that had been explored in the other papers, arguing very strongly that a linear understanding of dialogue and togetherness cannot be as fruitful as the understanding that a circular and less predictable way of journeying together could bring a more fruitful journey.

At this point in the conference, a participant who had been supporting the movement for the Christian ordination of women challenged the stance of a circular, metaphysical and infinite way of dealing with the problem, as she put it, of the religious traditions and their resistance to change. She had a point, and she challenged the stance of the conference on silence as complicity. The point was well taken within the possibilities and need for change within Christian traditions. However, the response by the Hindus was firm and challenging. It reminded me of the responses to Western educational and charity initiatives within India at times when Indians have challenged some of the European involvements within poverty and rights in India as neo-colonial. I understand that these are complex issues; however, exchanges about difficult issues in development, theology and interfaith dialogue need to be faced rather than avoided.

The dialogue between this European theologian and a Hindu practitioner brings the crux of the gulf to be bridged within a mutual conversation. For in Europe time is linear and the objectives of an orderly God are somehow mixed with our own sense of linear security. Utterances provide an expression to thought, and it is thought that can bring action, while action can bring a solution to an impasse. The message and response by the Hindu practitioner was to assume that we do not know what will happen, because in a circular time and space the relatedness of all, including the cosmos, does not give the centrality to one answer and many answers can arise. The chanting of a mantra can affect the energies that are interacting and providing action beyond our understanding.

I would have preferred this intervention by the European theologian not to have taken place because it distracted us for a few minutes from the desire to listen to each other. In terms of what had been happening at the signing and during that morning, the voice of a European theologian violently pushed for the noise and the hurrying of doing, arguing that there was little time left in this life to address a problem of inequality and find a solution. The Hindu understanding of the ongoing reincarnation where there is no end contradicted completely the hurriedness of a Greco-Roman world. Inadvertently the conversation in silence called for a different language in which both worlds could at least listen to each other. The day after the signing of the Declaration was a conference day in which thoughts were uttered. I was glad of the exchanges, but I was happier when Sunday arrived.

On the Sunday and at Parliament Hall, an old room where the Scottish parliament was in session for a few years, there was an hour that participants could use to pray, meditate and be in silence, regardless if they were Christians, Buddhists or Hindus. There was no introduction or guidance, and while Kabir Babu sat on the floor to meditate those who were less used to public prayer sat at the back of the room, probably wondering what was going to happen. Those attending the meditation proceeded together to the University Chapel, where every Sunday at 11.00am there is an ecumenical Christian service. For the Hindus, this was the first time they had attended a Christian service within a Christian chapel. For most of the Christians this was the first time that they had prayed together with Hindus and Buddhists.

It can be done, and I insist, in my opinion, that dialogue is reciprocal so that, as I have visited Hindu and Buddhist places of worship in India, this was the time for the Indian delegation to attend a Christian service. After the service, we proceeded to St Andrews Pier, and at the steps where the boats arrive Kabir Babu led us onto the chanting of the OM. *India we greet you!* This was the thought in our hearts, as in a line there were Hindus, Christians and Buddhists praying together with the unity and the unison of the OM that dominates all levels of existence and makes the sounding of creation resonate with unity. I could only remember that for Henri Le Saux the OM was the only necessary sound that finally silenced all other prayers and sounds.

This chanting of the OM marked the end of the conference but not the end of dialogue, as Ramesh, Kabir and I headed for a short visit to Arunachala Hermitage in Anstruther and for conversations on the Pier. We had left the thought-filled conference, and we had returned to our own dialogue which had previously taken place in Amritsar. I shared with them a brief outline of my daily routine and meditation at the hermitage, and

Ramesh shared his own metaphysical language and his reflections. Once again, as it had been in Amritsar, the conversation was focused through the reading of a poem he had written one night when he awoke and was not sure if he was alive or dead. 'The Night of the Dead', originally written in Hindi, conveyed his own sharing of a journey in which an ongoing commonality in dialogue can take place at the moment of death and the beyond. If we live intensively, we prepare ourselves for death and judgement in Christianity, and for death and reincarnation in Hinduism. I reflect on death in the last chapter of this work, because death becomes a vehicle of understanding between Christianity and Hinduism. Death offers the possibilities of feeling a togetherness in mystery, in fear, in hope and in expectation, because what others have taught us will only become clear at the moment of our death.

However, what I want to emphasize at the end of this chapter is the natural development of a different language in dialogue, that of mysticism and silence on the one hand, and the language of the heart and the imagination on the other. Poetry, music and dance become vehicles of expression for this human commonality in dialogue, which cannot be comprehended or expressed through the rational understanding of a common given. Such a given does not exist because a Christian and a Hindu have different explanations for beginning and end and for a human and divine pilgrimage in general. The language of a poem is the language of the soul longing to express unexpressed realities to receive a response from others. Thus it is clear that, within this ongoing dialogue, the silence of a hermit and the creativity of poets have successfully mediated any untold differences because silence and poetry have expressed the longing of a soul for another beyond words, beyond fights, beyond history and beyond canons.

In the following chapter I explore elements for Christian liturgies that can foster prayer and dialogue between Christians and Hindus.

Chapter 4

CREATING LITURGIES FOR THE ABSOLUTE

One of the qualities and characteristics of the cenobium, that is of the monastic orders who live in community such as the Benedictines, has been the development of liturgical hymns and liturgical orders to be used within the common office.[1] Such orders have enriched the liturgy of the Church through the seven daily offices and the daily celebration of the Eucharist.[2] The Gregorian chanting of the cenobitic communities has been an example of daily prayer and contemplation, and the hermitages, originally extensions of monasteries, were recipients of such liturgical developments in the East and in the West.[3] Those monks who pioneered the encounter between Christianity and Hinduism had to ask questions about the possibilities and opportunities that arose after Vatican II. One of them, Abhishiktananda, asked particular questions regarding the relation between Christian liturgy and Indian symbols and traditional rites.[4] In Panikkar's assessment it was because 'he alone, who has assimilated tradition at its best, can go beyond it'.[5] Bede Griffiths developed forms of Eucharistic celebration and liturgical inculturation that incurred critical comments by Indian liturgists, clergy and bishops.[6] However, an agreement that settled all discussions and experimentations and provided a step forward was the acceptance of a common Indian rite by the 1980s. The Indian rite for the celebration of the Eucharist was used at Shantivanam, the hermitage founded by Monchanin and Le Saux, where Bede Griffiths settled after Abhishiktananda decided to become a hermit in northern India.[7]

This chapter reflects on some of those liturgical developments and tries to develop liturgies and prayers for a hermitage of the twenty-first century (see appendices). It argues that one of the possibilities of praying together is not only to exercise the presence of others within a hermitage but also to join others' moments of prayer from time to time in different settings and in silence through the internet.

EREMITICAL LITURGIES

The importance of the liturgy and the centrality of the celebration of the Eucharist within the Catholic Church must not be underestimated.[8] Thus it was no surprise that the first Constitution approved by Vatican II was the Constitution on the Liturgy (*Sacrosanctum Concilium* – SC) on 4 December 1963, five years earlier than Fr Bede Griffiths' arrival at Shantivanam. The importance of the liturgy and the Eucharist was outlined at the start of the document: 'for it is the liturgy through which, especially in the divine sacrifice of the Eucharist, "the work of our redemption is accomplished"' (SC 2). Within such reaffirmation to the faithful, Vatican II outlined the need to revise the liturgical rites, stating that 'the Council also desires that, where necessary, the rites be revised carefully in the light of sound tradition, and that they be given new vigour to meet present-day circumstances and needs' (SC 4). In chapter I.3 the liturgical reform was outlined, stating that within the liturgy there are 'unchangeable elements divinely instituted' and 'elements subject to change' (SC 21). Two general assumptions guided this renewal of the liturgy, namely that 'texts and rites should be drawn up so as to express more clearly the holy things which they signify' and that Christian people 'should be able to understand them with ease and take part in them fully, actively, and as a community' (SC 21). The changes in the spirit of the liturgy were the result of the deliberations of bishops from all over the world that were empowered to explore the difficult area of 'unchangeable elements divinely instituted' and 'elements subject to change' (SC 21).

Bede Griffiths and all the other pioneers were aware that in their personal judgement of elements to be incorporated within the Eucharist they needed to exercise a cautious imaginary action: to decide what they sought fit to do and to match that with the possible permission needed by the local bishop. However, as the period after Vatican II was certainly perceived as a period of experimentation throughout the Catholic Church, there was room for such experimentation, an opportunity that was fully taken by Bede Griffiths.[9] Any description of the liturgy at Shantivanam by his biographers and those who were there over the years shows a progression in liturgical adaptation *ad experimentum* which started during the early 1970s. Some elements of the start of the Mass and the offertory were enriched by Hindu texts, chanting and symbols, keeping in line with what Vatican II had argued had to be maintained, that is the Eucharistic prayer and the consecration ('unchangeable elements', SC 21). After the publication of the new Roman Missal in 1972, the Vatican sent a circular letter in 1973 suggesting that the period of experimentation between the end of Vatican II and 1972 had been quite productive. Some of those liturgical experiments had been conducted on the creation and use of new Eucharistic Prayers; however, only a few of those experiments were taken as possible avenues for liturgical celebrations by the Vatican. To that effect the Sacred Congregation for Divine Worship stated clearly that 'there are at present four Eucharistic prayers, those in the revised Roman Missal. It is not permissible to use any other Eucharistic Prayer which has not been composed by permission of the Holy See or approved by it.'[10] With those words the period of liturgical adaptation and experimentation came to an end, while local churches continued to explore the liturgical possibilities offered by their own contexts.

One of the most widely used experimental Eucharistic Prayers was the Indian Eucharistic Prayer drawn up by Fr Dr D.S. Amalorpavadass of the National Biblical Catechetical Centre, Bangalore, with a group of Indian liturgists in the early 1970s.[11] The IV All India Liturgical Meeting that took place in Bangalore in December 1973 stated that

> while a start has already been made towards the creation of new liturgical texts, it is of vital importance that efforts in this direction be continued and intensified...this requires that we enter into dialogue with men of other faiths and that we are prepared to learn from their religious experience.[12]

The Indian Eucharistic Prayer ended with the congregation's response – OM, TAT, SAT – following an inculturated text of the great Amen that concluded the Eucharistic Prayer:

> Celebrant: In the Oneness of the Supreme Spirit through Christ who unites all things in his fullness we and the whole creation give to you, God of all, Father of all, honour and glory, thanks and praise, worship and adoration, now and in every age, for ever and ever.

> Congregation: Amen. You are the fullness of reality, one without a second, being, knowledge, bliss! OM, TAT, SAT![13]

Years later, and after the appointment of Cardinal Knox to the Congregation for Divine Worship and the Discipline of the Sacraments (1974–1983) at the Vatican, this experimental Eucharistic Prayer was no longer permitted to be used within the Eucharistic celebrations in India.[14] Nevertheless, India remained a fruitful seed for liturgical inculturation, as it had been since the time of the arrival of the Jesuits in the sixteenth century.[15]

In the case of Bede Griffiths, liturgical adaptations to India and the use of texts from other world religions for daily prayer at Shantivanam Ashram continued in earnest. Thomas Matus, a Camaldolese Benedictine who lived with Bede Griffiths in the 1980s, has provided an accurate description of the celebration of this 'Indian Rite' at Shantivanam:

> The priest says all the prescribed prayers of the Roman Missal, but he and the other participants sit yoga-style on the floor. Concelebrating priests drape an orange-coloured shawl around their shoulders in lieu of a stole and chasuble. The preparation of bread and wine at the offertory is embellished by the 'sacrifice of the elements' – water, earth (flowers), air (incense), and fire, as in the Hindu rites of puja.[16]

If Bede Griffiths did not have an outright prohibition from liturgical experimentation by his local bishop, it was because his liturgical adaptations were celebrated only within the ashram and nowhere else.

In providing some thoughts on liturgical symbols and prayers used at Arunachala Hermitage today, I dwell on the same principle of cautiousness and respect for the Roman Rite that Bede Griffiths exercised. Thus, in drawing liturgies for the communication with the Absolute today, it is necessary to understand the first difference between Christianity and Hinduism located in the variety of religious experiences. The sense of symbolic existences and symbolism provokes a unity of purpose in which, as there are many Hinduisms, there are many forms of Christianity. The Self within daily prayer as a unique manifestation of identity becomes a communal Self of common identity in which the Self represents manifestations of the divine creation within Christianity and of the self-realization of an ongoing truth within Hinduism. Bede Griffiths used Indian forms for the liturgy, meaning symbols that would make Christian liturgies more accessible to the cultural context of India in the manner of liturgies and theologies of inculturation. A communal liturgy as witnessed by Thomas Matus was a compromise between what he intended to move forward and the traditional rejection of Hindu forms by Catholic clergy in India. In a more eremitical way Abhishiktananda departed from searching for a communal way and developed a self-centred way of prayer that left behind forms and actions as an ongoing preoccupation and dwelt with the silence of the departure from the duality of space and time. Thus, as was the case with Abhishiktananda, prayer centred on the self and the absence of material forms does not provide a challenge to liturgies of inculturation or the celebration of the Eucharist and prayer moments within the communal setting of parishes or Christian communities.

Liturgies and prayers developed within a hermitage in the twenty-first century have been heavily influenced by these pioneers. Therefore, and without contradiction, it is possible to develop liturgies and prayers that incorporate Indian forms in the communal sense and to develop a more silent and non-dualistic sense of personal and individual prayer and meditation. These forms of prayer incorporate *Advāita Vedānta* as a Hindu form of understanding that brings Christian hermits and Hindu *sadhus* closer to each other, if not in space at least in time and form. As a result, a deep love for a common path between Christian hermits and Hindu renouncers can evolve, showing deep respect towards each other in the manner that Abhishiktananda developed. For, at the start of his exodus from Shantivanam, he wrote: 'Let us plunge into the depth of India in the name of the Church, and there discover Christ the Purusha, for he more truly pre-exists in the Purusha than in the Greek Logos and awaits his unveiling.'[17]

In the following paragraphs, I explore some elements, moments and movements that become important to actualize the togetherness of Christians and Hindus within the daily prayer at Arunachala Hermitage.

ELEMENTS, MOMENTS AND MOVEMENTS
THE MORNING SEATING

Can I sit on the floor with my brothers and sisters? Some Roman liturgists objected in the past because it was not culturally Roman or European to sit on the ground. The absence of furniture at Arunachala Hermitage, of comfortable sofas and cushions for prayer, witnesses to the unity with India where most people sit on the floor. It also witnesses to the communion of renunciation with the poor and the marginalized, as was the case of Saint Theresa of Calcutta (1910–1997), who instructed her nuns to pray sitting on the floor and in front of the Blessed Sacrament. The first movement for the morning prayer is to sit side by side on the ground with the hands saluting the rising of the sun or the breaking of the day. The hands close to the chest, the mouth and the forehead bowing to the Absolute, taking in the beauty of the morning, the rays of light that shower upon Christians and Hindus alike, the rays of the Risen Christ who shines over all humanity, the fire of the morning that extends through the sun not to some but to all sentient beings. In those first moments of the morning I take a few moments to become aware of creation and of the communion between my space and those occupied by Christians and Hindus elsewhere.

> *I sit on the floor aware of the light*
> *I sit on the floor aware of my Hindu brothers and sisters*
> *I sit on the floor greeting the morning and the Lord!*
> *Let the hymns to Christ and to Shiva resound!*
> *Let the Amen and the OM resound together!*
> *Let the sun shine on Christians and Hindus*
> *Let the Peace that surpasses all understanding reign*
> *Let visions of the Ganges and of Jerusalem shine upon us!*
> *Amen. OM TAT TA.*[18]

It is the ground, the bare ground, that unites all humanity because all of us are standing or sitting on it. All chairs and pews are different and reflect poverty or riches. However, every morning it is on the ground that Christians and Hindus pray at the rising of the sun after a few drops of water have refreshed our senses and even when water is not available. The pious Hindus recite, at the rising of the sun, the Gayatri Mantra or the Savitri Mantra: *tat savitur varenyem bhargo devasya dhimahi dhiyo yo nah prachodayat* – Let us meditate on this beloved light of the god who enlivens. May he inspire our thoughts.[19]

The mind is focused on the pointed meditation until it opens to the quality of silence. For it is in silence that the mediation of *nada* (nothing) in the words of Panikkar brings the creativity of the presence of the self. It is within such awareness, in calmness and stillness, that silence creates the possibility of union and communion with other places and other peoples.[20] The empty mind becomes filled with the silence of the union between this space and the other space, united by time. It is within this first sitting that the cosmos becomes united with a world without beginning and without end. The minutes in silence pass without consciousness of a short time or a long time, but time becomes Being, as silence cannot be isolated from Being, because it is through Being that silence is experimented.

THE MORNING PROSTRATION

The act of prostration, in common terms to be 'flat on the ground', is used within the liturgical rites of the Catholic Church at the start of the liturgy of Good Friday. The priest enters the church with an empty altar as the Blessed Sacrament has been removed to an altar of repose the previous evening. The altar has been completely stripped of altar cloths, candles and other ornamentations. In front of the cross the priest prostrates on the ground, joining the Lord who is ritually remembered as being not among the living and not among the saints but who dies and goes deep into the place of the dead to rise from the dead at the Easter Vigil. The red stole and vestments complete a ritual moment that moves the faithful because at very few times in our lives do Christians prostrate on the ground. The other occasion within the Catholic ritual year in which prostration takes place is within the Rite of Ordination of Priests. The candidate for ordination prostrates while the Litany of the Saints is chanted or recited. The candidate rises in order to receive the imposition of hands by the ordaining bishop and all other priests present. For, 'if to bless means to adore, blessing and adoration are documented in Scripture by prostration and the physical bending of the knee and, metaphysically, of the heart'.[21]

It is a very humbling experience to be on the ground, and it reminds us of our position of servants and creatures in front of a divine majestic divine force and presence. Tibetan Buddhists prostrate quite often in temples and sacred places, and their prostrations connect them with the sacred grounds of a temple or a stupa and with the materiality of being on the ground. One prostration starts where the other ended, where the hands extended on the ground have reached, so that the prostrations lead the 'walking' of the pilgrims, who advance through the landscape prostrating rather than walking on their two feet.

When I prostrate in the morning before and after the morning seating, I connect myself with the past, the present and the future. In the past, and during the ritual in which I was ordained as a Catholic priest, I prostrated on the ground of the chapel of the school where I had studied for 12 years, primary and secondary school, in order to prepare for the imposition of hands by the Chilean bishop Manuel Camilo Vial. In the past I have prostrated at the Buddhist temples of Dharamsala with Tibetan monks who have enthusiastically felt a full communion in silence whenever we prostrated on that ground where so many others have prostrated before us. The sign of respect for the past that I propose can occur every morning after the pointed meditation. The past becomes the present and the future, because on prostrating we remember that we are creatures with all other human beings and all other sentient beings.

The Eucharist

For many Catholic priests it is customary to celebrate the Eucharist daily. If within monastic communities and parishes the celebration of the Eucharist follows the same norms and patterns of the Roman Missal, I am proposing to use other elements in order to express communion with Hindus and Buddhists when one is on one's own. New elements and the possible changes within the liturgy have been a point of contention and worry for liturgists since the experimentation that followed Vatican II. My sense is that, within a hermitage, there is only one person worshipping God and celebrating the liturgy for the benefit of others who have asked for prayers and to be remembered in their own pilgrimage.

As is the custom within the monastic communities, the celebration of the Eucharist follows a period of *lectio divina*, of reading of texts that can inspire and guide the life of the monks. *Lectio divina* is not just an intellectual reading and a reading that provides knowledge of texts, but a detailed dwelling within the space of the text. In faith, the reader contacts God through the text and learns slowly in prayer, examining each sentence and letting the heart speak to God, about God and to God. Texts from the Bible, especially from the Psalms, are particularly useful for these periods of *lectio divina*. Monastic communities also use the Fathers of the Church, selections of which are usually included in the Office of Readings, the first office of the day within the seven offices included within the Roman breviary. For example, Tertullian's *On Prayer* becomes a source of *lectio*, which can help the reader to become closer to God, once read line by line. The resonance of the wise words and experience of Tertullian becomes an aid to love God better during that morning period before the celebration of the Eucharist.

It is a fact that the advent of the internet has provided resources for everyone while, at the time of Thomas Merton, for example, texts from the Fathers had to be accessed in their original language, in this case Latin. Those texts were translated and copied to whoever was reading, simply because the monastic books that had been copied were of a rather large size and not available to everyone. I have offered my own short *lectio* on the Upanishads and the Way of the Bodhisattva in the following chapter. On purpose, I have offered the reading of only a few verses of the works being read, following the historical tradition of the Cistercians, whereby only some verses are read and prayed over a long period of time. If all verses of a text were taken together this could distract the reader into the possibility of writing a textual and analytical commentary on the full text.

I follow the order for the celebration of the Eucharist in the Catholic Church (Roman Rite) that has the following moments within a general division in the Liturgy of the Word and the Liturgy of the Eucharist: welcoming, Lord Have Mercy, opening prayer, readings, prayers of the faithful, offertory, Eucharist Prayer with preface, 'Holy, Holy', and consecration, reciting of the 'Our Father', sign of peace, Lamb of God, communion, final prayer and blessing.

The celebration of the Eucharist always starts with the silence of the communion with other communities in India, and within those particularly with the Hindu and Buddhist communities. The Trinitarian formula that opens the celebration 'In the name of the Father, the Son and the Holy Spirit' provides a cosmic union that goes back in time before the foundation of the Church or in fact any religious tradition. In the words of Panikkar, 'the cosmotheandric experience "re-links" Man with the Divine as well as with the Cosmos and with his Humanity in a thematically stronger way than up to now'; thus religion (*religare*) relinks Man with himself, with society, with the earth and with the Divine.[22] The non-dualistic understanding provided by Panikkar links the Eucharist immediately at its very start with the whole of God's creation in one, because even the start of a particular celebration of the Eucharist is no more than the continuation of all previous ones and the start of all the celebrations that will follow until eternity.

The Lord Have Mercy that follows integrates the prayer of mercy for moments in which the inhumanity of humans has provided a catastrophe of selfishness and death. Thus in the last chapter of this work I expand the context and content of Pope Francis' visit to Auschwitz. Pope Francis' cry 'Lord, have mercy on your people! Lord, forgiveness for so much cruelty!' expands itself in every daily 'Lord Have Mercy' within the Eucharist at the hermitage. Moments of holocaust, genocide and mass murder remind us of the communion in sinfulness and despair with those who have been killed, who in most cases do not have a name, a history or even a tomb to remember them. Thus tragic events such as the Shoah remind us of the suffering of the Jewish people, while the memory of the killing of Muslims and Hindus during the period of partition in India reminds us of the religious hatred that can be present in our common humanity. Memories of the Rwanda genocide make us cry 'Lord Have Mercy', because one million Rwandans, who were all united in a common faith, were slaughtered under the false banner of ethnic divisions and narratives of inclusion/exclusion that do not have a place within the Christian faith. The killing fields of Cambodia or the genocide of Tibetans reminds us of the moments in which we ourselves feel hatred towards others, of the exclusion of immigrants and distrust of refugees and of people who are not like ourselves. It is always possible to read a passage of history related to any of these dark moments in history before exclaiming, like Pope Francis, 'Lord, have mercy on your people! Lord, forgiveness for so much cruelty!'

The readings within the Eucharist celebration could be composed of a mixture from different traditions or the rotation between traditions so that a Christian reading is read one day, a Hindu reading the following day and a Buddhist reading on the third day. I propose the following examples to start with:

Even as a spider sends forth and draws in its threat, even as plants arise from the earth and hairs from the body of man, even so the whole creation arises from the Eternal.[23]

For sentient beings, poor and destitute, may I become a treasure ever-plentiful, and lie before them closely in their reach, a varied source of all that they might need.[24]

For when he dies, and they place him on the fire, then he is born out of the fire, and then the fire consumes only his body. And just as he is born from his father or from his mother, in that very way he is born from the fire.[25]

These readings could be taken as the first reading with silence after, or with the chanting of the OM, or with a chanted psalm, followed by the reading of the Gospel of the day. After a period of silence and meditation, the prayers for the Church, Hindus and Buddhists follow, with the suggestion that the names of those who have asked for prayers be placed on a paper in a bowl and, at this moment of universal prayer, be burned with a candle so that the flames and the smoke bring their names into the atmosphere, into the air that I breathe, that after all is connected with the air of the whole planet, the air of common humanity. It was Bede Griffiths who, following the initial ideas of the founders of Shantivanam, developed these ideas in liturgical practice with the understanding that 'Jesus restored humanity, not only Jews or Christians or any other particular group, to that oneness'.[26]

As it was done at Shantivanam, 'the preparation of bread and wine at the offertory is embellished by the "sacrifice of the elements" – water, earth (flowers), air (incense), and fire, as in the Hindu rites of puja'.[27] The elements are acknowledged on the altar with the water being sprinkled on the elements with the tips of the fingers, the flowers and the air being sanctified with the fire. The flower symbolizes the ultimate divinity – that divinity that one tries to reach: 'the flower floats in the middle of the primordial waters, drifting from shore to shore...it has no roots in this world'.[28] That fire could be a match, a bowl with a candle in, or even a candle that is lifted and moved around the elements with piety and veneration. It is at that moment that the unity takes place with Hindus who are performing the fire ceremony, with Buddhists who are burning candles to the Lord Buddha in their temples, with Christians all over the world and, indeed, with the whole of humanity.

It is the fire that becomes at all times within the liturgy of the day the link between the light of Christ and the daily Hindu rituals in which fire is used. Agni, the god of fire, appears and is invoked at the beginning of the Rig Veda, a deity that brings the oblation from humans to the gods, intercedes between human and gods and brings the gods to the sacrifice. Thus, the beginning of the Rig Veda: 'I pray to Agni, the household priest who is the god of the sacrifice, the one who chants and invokes and brings most treasure.'[29] Within this practice the building of a fire altar is the responsibility of every householder, and within this practice three fires are to be maintained: the household fire, the ceremonial fire and the sacrificial fire.[30]

The offertory provides the possibility of using elements that bring together the form and symbol of the five elements related to Hinduism and the memory of Jesus and his use of elements that Jews used for a meal with friends, namely bread and wine. I would suggest in the ongoing continuity with contextual forms that bread and wine could be substituted for the elements used in India by most people for a meal and that resonates with other countries of the third, fourth and fifth world where wine is a luxury, a foreign product to be imported. Thus, bread used as unleavened bread within the Passover meal and of a particular wheat form within Europe could be substituted by one of the breads of India. The most common bread, the bread of the poor found in every market and on every cooking stove in India, is the chapatti. While wine is a European luxury, clean water is also a luxury for many in India and, indeed, in Asia, and clean water could be the drink provided for the celebration of this

Eucharistic meal. Thus the eating of chapattis and the drinking of clean water speak of a heavenly feast.

The 'Holy, Holy' resembles the possibility of the eternal adoration that the Absolute Divinity, the Trinity in its cosmic unity, deserves, with the bells, the incense and the chanting that accompany the joyful processions of the divine joy and the divine acceptance. It is within this moment, an extended one with clouds of incense, that the fire ceremony seems appropriate because it is here that the tradition of the sacrificial fires reverberates with the absolute throng of angels and archangels that sing the praises of God for eternity.

The Eucharistic Prayer continues with the memorial of the Last Supper in which Jesus prepares the eternal banquet in which all are welcome. The importance of meals served within Hindu feasts and of the eating and drinking tea within *pujas* resonate here. There is no absolute separation between the sharing of tea, bread and jam during a Buddhist *puja* and the intense prayers, chants, meditation, prostrations and reading of texts. Here a practical detail arises that needs to be reflected on: the issue of fasting before receiving the Eucharist and the eating within a Buddhist *puja*. During a *puja* in Dharamsala at a nunnery, I had requested that a text from Tsong Kapa be read or chanted. The text was chanted to my joy, as it was a special *puja* for my life companion and myself. However, after the chanting, tea was served in cups located in front of our small tables as we were sitting on the floor. Nuns themselves took their cups and received the warm liquid from large kettles in which the tea with abundant milk and sugar had been boiled. Prayers continued and naan breads with jam were also shared around. Each nun received a large naan bread while prayers continued. My reflection was that within the very harsh climate of the lower Himalayas, which are covered in snow in winter, and a temple which had open doors and very thin windows, this was a very wise practice. After all, it did not interfere with the prayers being said; on the contrary it secured the possibility that those praying could stay longer. Two years later, while at the Golden Temple in Amritsar, I was reminded of this very nice custom as pilgrims were offered sweet rice and water as they were walking and praying around the holy waters of the Temple. I leave it to the reader to make the informed choice regarding drinking tea while praying, but it is a custom of Asia that on dark days and showery February days has been a possibility in the winter climate of Scotland.

The great Amen after the Eucharistic Prayer remains a central moment in which the Amen and the OM of all humanity cries in unison to the absolute glory of the Absolute. The prayer for peace and the sign of peace that follows unites the hermitage with the universal presence of the Absolute in that my greetings go not to the absent human beings within the hermitage but towards the rest of humanity and towards all sentient beings. Indeed, the fire and energy that arises out of that prayer, 'Peace be with you', reminds us that the energy arises out of a moment of meditation in which in the words of the Upanishads 'by *Tapas*, the power of meditation, Brahman attains expansion and then comes primeval matter'.[31]

The reception of the Eucharist in bread and wine, chapatti and water, brings God to us and to the rest of humanity, and so we pray for all at the end of the Eucharist:

> *May this Eucharist bring joy and peace to all*
> *humanity and to all sentient beings.*
> *May the Lord who provides full understanding*
> *empty our minds to a new humanity.*
> *May the unity of the Trinity bring forth in all of us the*
> *unity of humanity and the whole of creation.*
> *May we be the bridge and the raft for all those*
> *who suffer. Amen. OM TAT TA.*

THE EVENING FIRE

In the evening we sit on the ground in silence beside the fire. With such silence the lighting of a candle reminds us that the night is upon us, and we give thanks for those we have encountered during the day. Once again we send energy to those who suffer through the lighting of the fire and the silence that follows, in which the energy of our prayers could bring God closer to those who need his presence more. It is possible to tune into those Hindus who are performing the fire ceremony in India, for example in Varanasi, through the internet. The fire ceremony is performed in the morning and in the evening, and it is a good manner to be in communion with Hindus in silence. After silent meditation, the recitation of Psalm 90, the psalm used within the breviary for night prayer, reminds us of the protection of the Lord for the night rest.

The evening brings with it the arrival of the night, and tired bodies search for rest and communion rather than possible action and energy. The possibilities of silence arise as shadows of the day, knowing that for Christians and Hindus the light of the morning and the light of the evening have different qualities, different experiences, but the same cyclical endless form and materiality.

THE LITURGICAL VISIT

On 26 July 2016 two men armed with knives took hostages at the church of Saint-Etienne-du-Rouvray in the French diocese of Rouen. The attackers killed Fr Jacque Hamel, aged 86, who was presiding over the Eucharist, by slashing his throat, and seriously injured another hostage. Pope Francis was 'particularly troubled to learn that this act of violence took place in a church, during Mass, a liturgical act that implores of God His peace on earth'.[32] The murder of the priest was condemned by Muslims in France, and some of them refused to bury the attacker shot dead by the police. On 31 July 2016, Muslims across France attended

Mass in a gesture of solidarity after the murder of Fr Hamel.[33] French Catholics were deeply moved by this act of solidarity and expressed their wish that the two religious communities could journey together hand in hand in peace and against all acts of terrorism that could divide them.

I would suggest that this act of visiting other faiths' places of worship is also a possibility for showing that we journey together and to experience such a journey. This is the basis of any dialogue: a deep respect for other ways of worshipping the Absolute, recognizing with Panikkar that 'whoever perceives the presence of God will respect everything and everybody; he will have, on the one hand, an extraordinary boldness and, on the other hand, an extreme diffidence'.[34] It is within such visits that we understand differences; however, instead of trying to comprehend intellectually the meaning of symbols and actions, as if we were students of world religion, we must experience prayer, silence and respect. The silence that gladdens the heart provides a unity with others that no conference or lecture can provide, and it is within those moments of visiting and of praying within somebody else's space that we become changed into agents of change and peace.

The extensions of an eremitic life provide the possibilities of welcoming others for silent prayer in ways which have not been used very much in a Western context.[35] However, in moments of need and joy, communities have come together to pray and to take actions to alleviate suffering and mistrust. Thus, on 30 July 2016, in the context of his visit to Poland, Pope Francis stopped at the Church of Saint Francis in Krakow. The church has relics of two Franciscan martyrs killed by the Peruvian 'Shining Path' guerrillas (Pariacoto, 9 August 1991), and Pope Francis recited a 'prayer for peace and protection from violence and from terrorism'.[36] The thirst for togetherness of the victims of terrorism towards others is expressed in the prayer's following words:

> Holy Spirit Consoler, visit the families of the victims of terrorism, families that suffer through no fault of their own. Wrap them in the mantle of Your divine mercy. Make them find again in You and in themselves the strength and courage to continue to be brothers and sisters for others, above all for immigrants, giving witness to Your love by their lives.[37]

If these visits make sense during moments of violence or natural disasters in which local communities work together for the common good, the visit to another faith's holy places or the participation in rituals awakens the centrality of prayer together. Prayer and meditation in silence become a central pillar for each other's appreciation and for understanding the common journey and common humanity. Every visit will make our journey of experimentation with the divine and the self concretely new because, after all, our own journey cannot be reproduced by somebody else. Experimentation gives us a sense of fear because we want to reach where we are supposed to be, and by experimenting we don't know if we are actually going to get to the right place. This fear creates the division between what we are about to be and what we never are, because the possibilities of the journey are crushed by a limited amount of experimentation. I agree with Panikkar's argument in which he suggests that 'the distinctions between experience, observation, and experiment should not be understood as separations'.[38]

In the following chapter I transcribe a *lectio divina* of non-Christian texts in order to show the possibility of a deep respect and appreciation for Hindu and Buddhist scriptures within a Christian journey and as an extension of the daily ritual practices of Arunachala Hermitage in Scotland.

Chapter 5

READING TEXTS

Upanishads and Bodhisattvas

In the previous chapter I outlined the possibilities of a diverse richness within the daily liturgy that in a hermitage connects heaven and earth through prayer and contemplation. In this chapter I explore the use of texts within the life of a hermit. I fully agree with the possibility that a simple sentence or a mantra is all that a hermit needs. I am reminded of Abhishiktananda's final discovery after many tensions and many daily searches: 'OM. This eternal word is all: what was, what is and what shall be, and what beyond is in eternity. All is OM.'[1]

One of the most important monastic activities of a hermit is the *lectio divina*, a mindful and prayerful reading of texts, that has usually been associated with the reading of texts from the Gospels, the Bible, and the Fathers of the Church.[2] It is a time (30–60 minutes) in which a human being searches for God and invites God to come to this moment. It is a prayerful reading in which phrases, words and sentences are read again and again in order to move them deeper into the heart. It reminds me of that ancient Tibetan custom by which a person reading or studying ancient texts has at all times a praying monk that accompanies such activity, so that it becomes a spiritual activity rather than an intellectual one. Thus, the ongoing recitation of the OM MANI PADME HUM aids the reader to become one with the words that are being read, as a teacher places the text on his forehead before and after uttering an explanation of the text being read, prayed and studied.

Thus, within the Christian tradition, *lectio divina* has emphasized the reading and study of the biblical text, very often taking the daily readings of the liturgy to prepare for such liturgical celebration. However, I would suggest accompanying such preparation for the liturgy with the daily reading of a text from another religious tradition as well. To read a text over a period, maybe a year, in which chapters are taken for a period of time, without hurry, without checking that I have read whatever I intended to read, could bring a further closeness to Buddhism or Hinduism. As the common readings of the daily liturgy make us feel in communion with all others celebrating the daily liturgy, the daily reading of other traditions' texts could bring that sense of experiencing a common journey despite being very far away in physical terms. This period of *lectio divina* is a period in which a text is taken deeper and longer than ever so that the heart opens and the love for God and neighbour burns and aches oneself. The addition of other texts elongates the possibilities of a journey and it elongates the period of reading texts. It is like the repetition of sentences again and again and again; for example: 'Jesus, Son of God, have mercy on me a sinner.' This sentence was repeated thousands of times by Bede Griffiths to calm a distracted mind and to focus on the prayer that could follow such a movement of the heart. However, a sentence from the Upanishads can also be taken as an opener to a longer period of reading. For example, 'by the path of good leads us to final bliss', 'deliver us from wandering evil' or 'prayers and adoration we offer unto thee'.[3]

I would argue that a period of *lectio divina* is a period of intense love for God and others, because the moment is not intended for one's own benefit only but the fire of the heart in intense motion and energy journeys to others, particularly those who need it. Following from the understanding that prayer, meditation and the generation of good energies touches others, the *lectio* is also a moment in which I embrace the poor, the marginalized and those rejected by society. This is a challenging thought because most Christian commentators have understood a hermit as a lone human being in prayer without emphasizing the connection of a hermit with those around the hermitage. It is clear in the life of Charles de Foucauld as well as in the history of the hermits in India that the two-fold commandment of loving God and neighbour is fully realized or at least thought about within the life of a hermit. The development of a hermitage brings daily a close connection with those around it, and soup, prayers, bread and a comforting word are part of a daily discipline of prayer and love of neighbour.[4]

Lectio divina incorporates the movements of a heart first rather than of the intellect, and the heart opens the avenues by which others become present in this complementary moment of being. For the mind follows the heart, and concentration in a moment in space and time frees from solely intellectual pursuits and opens the commonality of the mind with others. This is a religious experience in which the closer the hermit comes to God the closer other human beings are placed within the hermit's heart. It is plausible to argue that this movement from the heart to the mind and from emptiness to a mental embrace of those suffering and in need does not happen by chance. An example: today, as I was writing these words, having read in the morning, before leaving Nalanda Hermitage in Santiago, passages of the Dalai Lama's commentary on the Bodhicharyāvatāra, I saw a strange scene that was not a dream but reality.[5] I was leaving the Santiago Metro at Manuel Montt Station, and I saw a blind man whom I had seen many times over the previous years. However, this time he was crawling on the pavement. He usually begs for alms outside the Metro Station. He seemed to have difficulty in finding his white walking stick. I approached the scene and asked him if I should help him to stand. He told me to help him. I helped him stand and gave him his green plastic cup full of coins. I put some money in his cup and wished him luck.

His breath smelled of alcohol, although it was only midday. He was, I thought, a fellow human being. And questions came to my mind: How could I cope with being blind, if I were in his place? Was he being exploited by others who brought him to this location to beg for alms every day without his consent? Who was bringing him there? As he composed himself, he remained standing and wished me God's blessings. I continued walking knowing that this had been a sign that the *lectio divina* does not allow me to disappear from the world of those who are suffering hardship, of my fellow human beings, whatever their condition.

I propose to use other texts as well as Christian texts for *lectio divina*, especially my favourite Buddhist text and my favourite Hindu texts: the Bodhicharyāvatāra and the Upanishads.[6] But, first, I call to mind the beginning of John's Gospel, of which I have written previously, to understand that before human beings were created or had a particular way, a particular religion, there was the Trinity at the beginning, not of human time, but of universal and cosmic time.[7] I never liked this text when I was a political activist and a political prisoner, because I preferred Jesus and his whip turning tables at the temple in Jerusalem.[8] Forgive me if, in my later years and knowing that this is the second part of my human life, I have rediscovered the Trinity in that unity that brings me peace and a pointed meditation on their activities.[9] Maybe they talk to each other? Maybe the three persons resemble the unity and diversity of *brahman*? I don't know, but I feel closer to the Trinity in *lectio divina* than to the very active passages that triggered a missionary vocation in my younger years.[10]

The very first meditation that challenges the beginning in Christianity and Hinduism and that could provide an ongoing *lectio* for life is the beginning of the Gospel of John, and I transcribe my own *lectio* as follows:

John 1.1 – A meditation on the Gospel of John starts with the foundation of any Christology: 'In the beginning was the Word and the Word was with God.' This is the first stumbling block of any dialogue between Christians and Hindus. We Christians return to the beginning of creation, while Hindus do not have creation, they do not believe in a beginning. It is here that one must dwell longer in the sentence, because the Word was with God at the beginning. In this sentence the text does not suggest that the beginning of creation as we know it is the beginning of others or the beginning of the Word as an outspoken communication from God. God is at the beginning, and his Son is there and the Spirit hovering over the waters before creation. Thus, the Trinity is at the beginning, before any traces of humanity, animals or constellation of planets, or planet earth, are mentioned. It is at this beginning that we encounter the possibility of what the Upanishads consider the sitting beside in order to learn, to interiorize our common journey with others. For the Upanishads do not intend to solve our human problems but to reinforce the interior vision of a fully human person that can exit all suffering by being wise. The Upanishads propose sayings that come out of a situation in which the effort is made to end the material means of bridging the gods and humans. The Upanishads propose to go immediately, directly into the practice of meditation, of finding the absolute non-duality (*Advāita Vedānta*) in which symbols, signs and mediations are not at the centre any longer. It is within this sense of the non-duality and the secondary purpose of reality that the Upanishads meet with the central purpose of 'beyond' the *gate gate paragate* of the Buddha's realization. Go always beyond your understanding, says the Buddha, until the words and the explanation do not matter any longer. Within this realization Buddhists are active agents of help to others within the larger community and of respect of sentient beings and of the cosmos. It is within this encounter between the prayerful state of unity between the soul and the subconscious that the practitioner of meditation encounters the strength to respect others, to help them overcome suffering and to walk with others with absolute respect and joy.

THE CHALLENGE OF THE BODHICHARYĀVATĀRA

The Practice of the Bodhisattva Path was written by the monk Shantideva in the eighth century, and it constitutes one of the most loved texts of late Indian Buddhism.[11] Shantideva was a monk of royal birth of Nalanda monastery in northern India, who recited the text according to tradition when challenged to do something important as a monk. He responded to the challenge by teaching orally what we know as the Way of the Bodhisattva. While he was reciting he was being taken into the air during the recitation of the last part of the text. Therefore, there are two versions of the end of the text, as those who were listening heard different versions – some heard a shorter version, others a longer version.

Shantideva deals with a very difficult question within the life of a bodhisattva: how could a single human being free all beings in the universe from suffering? There were already opinions, verses, Mahayana sutras and poems regarding the bodhisattva. For example, the ideal of extreme charity had been outlined in the Shibi Jataka when King Shibi cut his own flesh to save the life of a dove. Exultations of a bodhisattva also appeared in the Avatamsaka Sutra. Shantideva's commitment to free other beings from suffering treats the bodhisattva vow seriously, not simply as words for prayer but as the guiding principle of the ordinary activities of one's life. I remember discussing the text with the Venerable Choje Lama Yeshe Losal Rimpoche, abbot and retreat master at the Kagyu Samye Ling (the Tibetan Buddhist Monastery in Scotland) after the signing of the St Andrews Declaration for a Shared Humanity. I had read a few verses of Shantideva's text during my opening speech and the abbot thanked me for that while remarking that one of the most difficult issues related to the text was to put it into practice.[12]

The text that provides a way of life for a bodhisattva also provides a link between meditation and emptiness and the general principles of the alleviation of suffering, bringing into full circle the possibilities of silence. It is worth mentioning that when Buddhism entered Tibet and reached its structural peak with the foundation of the monastic orders, very few undertook the radical path of the bodhisattva in practice, allowing for the diversification of practices and schools based on Tibetan clanship and social organization.[13] Thus, within the Geluk as the order of the Dalai Lamas, the text of the *Lam Rim Chen Mo* by Tsong Khapa, considered a Summa Theologica, and the second most important work in Tibetan Buddhism after the *Life of Milarepa*, became central for the bodhisattva path. In the *Lam Rim Chen Mo* Tsong Khapa introduced the notion of small, intermediate and great religious practitioners, whereby the notion of bodhicitta and the life of bodhisattva pertain only to those who are great religious practitioners.[14]

For it must be remembered that the impact of the way of the bodhisattva provided the actual practical way for those who achieved bodhicitta: they died as every other human being but returned to aid other beings rather than remaining in nirvana.[15] Thus, Shantideva's proposal of the daily alleviation of suffering created a link between the prayerful attitude of a bodhisattva and the 'bodhisattva deeds' later to be systematized in the theology of Tsong Khapa as the six perfections of giving, ethics, patience, effort, concentration and wisdom, with Tsong Khapa's emphasis on 'concentration' and 'wisdom'.

The guiding principle in understanding the possibilities and causes of silence within the Bodhicharyāvatāra is the principle of interdependence. Thus, the commentary by the 14th Dalai Lama on interdependence argues that 'everything we experience results from a complex interplay of causes and conditions, we find that there is no single thing to desire or resent, and it is more difficult for the afflictions of attachment or anger to arise'.[16] Silence becomes the guiding principle of the alleviation of suffering, not because it provides a reflexive moment in order to plan good actions or communal positive actions, but because it provides a way of life that starts with small actions towards other beings. In Buddhism, human beings, other sentient beings and the cosmos are all interconnected. Thus, the concern for animals and plants is only an extension of the interdependence of sentient beings, and the bodhisattva's intention to alleviate suffering.

> *The goal of every act is happiness itself,*
> *Though, even with great wealth, it's rarely found.*
> *So take your pleasure in the excellence of others.*
> *Let them be a heartfelt joy to you.[17]*

The *lectio* on the Bodhicharyāvatāra becomes a utopian and loving meditation on how to empty oneself of desires and ill thoughts to help others to do so themselves. The *lectio* brings a movement out of a hermitage, but centred within a hermitage, that goes towards others with a mind rather than a heart ready to change to help others achieve happiness, peacefulness and interconnectedness with others. The aim of happiness when others understand the causes and remedies for suffering becomes a personal cry in Shantideva's text to become such a mediator and helper to others. For sickness is not a material illness, but ignorance, and the bodhisattva can then become a healer, 'the doctor, nurse, the medicine itself'.[18] The guiding of others requires connecting with all sentient beings and explaining to them how the world operates, always knowing that they can heal themselves once they come out of ignorance, the not-knowing. For the interconnectedness of sentient beings and the cosmos relates quite closely with the Christian notion of neighbour, explained ad nauseam in many different categories, but at the end understood as all human beings and those created by God within a cosmos that is not ours but God's. For within

Shantideva's text my merits are not mine any longer; I can give them to others freely 'to bring about the benefits of beings'.[19]

The mind, then, within the *lectio* of Buddhist texts, becomes the vehicle for the awakening of a human being who in meditating and assuming a path is ready to help others. The *lectio* becomes an examination of a text that immediately brings the possibility of a meditative hermit who, in being still and empty, is ready not only to teach others but also to send energy and happiness to others. The final dedication of a bodhisattva brings that change in the possibilities that have arisen through *lectio* with the dedication that 'may I continue likewise to remain' 'to drive away the sorrows of the world'.[20]

The sorrows of the world combine the possibilities of negating the happiness that can embrace us when we leave the ignorance of solely trying to fulfil our potential through materiality. It is something else that brings the news, that Good News, alive. Without creating a tension between the material and the immaterial, the longing for material preoccupations makes Christians very unhappy. It is always the sign and symbol of those on a spiritual path that regardless of the challenges associated with such a path there is a peace and a joy that others admire. For example, before his death at age 55, away from India in the United States, Anthony de Mello SJ, the Jesuit who found connections between Christianity and Buddhism and who delighted international audiences with his stories, wrote to a friend: 'I don't know if this is an illusion; the only thing I know is that I have never in my life felt so happy and so free.'[21]

LECTIO WITH THE UPANISHADS

The Upanishads represent a reform within Hinduism and the end of the Veda. They are the final texts of the body of literature known as *shruti* ('what is heard'), as different from *smriti* ('what is remembered'). Thus, the nature of the Upanishads is divinely inspired. However, in case the reader feels any confusion, these texts are non-canonical, and they aim at guiding the path with the gods towards immortality. They are revered by Hindus because they explain the renunciation of so many holy men and women who bring blessings and holiness on others. However, as clearly stated by Hindus in Amritsar during our conversations in June 2016, they never studied the Upanishads formally, but they remember when they were children that holy men stopped to talk to them, and they recited some of them. The reading of the Upanishads always offered guiding principles to understand conversations that took place in foundational periods of Hinduism. Those new periods did not provide a challenge to previous understandings but they co-existed side by side. Thus, 'the Upanishads began as notes to the Brahmanas and as explanatory meditations of the Vedic rituals and myths'.[22]

> *Isa Upanishad* – 'Behold the universe in the glory of God:
> and all that lives and moves on earth. Leaving the transient,
> find joy in the Eternal: set not your heart on another's
> possession.'[23]

I take this text and read it all through first, then by paragraph, then line by line. The universe in the glory of God reminds me of the narrative of creation (Genesis 1) and the psalms that cry out the glory of God. However, I am immediately conscious that I read to meditate and I have contemplated the beauty of God's creation many times. Hinduism does not have a moment of initial creation, and therefore the meaning and feeling for the text must go further than just the relation with a creator God. The universe in the glory of God and all that lives and moves on earth speaks of the interconnectedness of all creation with each other, of the Hindu cosmos in which we move, of the Buddhist relation between all sentient beings and creation. 'Leaving the transient, find joy in the Eternal.' I find here what I want, which is the necessary movement from the material to the Eternal, to the silenced sound that speaks within that period and space in which I close my eyes and I withdraw my sentiments and feelings to be with the Eternal, or should I say to be in the Eternal. A moment that has been classified and innovated once and again over years, the joyful moment in which in the Eternal I find peace, I find sorrow, I find the nothingness of the moment to be, of the moment of existence that leaves behind all cosmic feeling but that at the same time connects me with all the cosmic melody of the universe. I am reminded of the hymns of poetry and joy cried out by Latin American poets such as Ernesto Cardenal and Nicanor Parra, poets and scientists expressing the form, colour and shapes of molecules and planets, the interconnected sense of the cosmos together.[24] The encounter between Nicanor Parra and Thomas Merton in which they digressed about matter and spirit while Merton was in love with feelings towards nurse M – in secret, in confidence, but in joy.[25] A certain togetherness of the different universes in which the joy is expressed by the moment, the second, the hour in which I find joy in the Eternal and I do not set my heart on another's possession. A moment that ends as I end but remains within the eternity of the circular mystery of silence and of human beings belonging to different traditions that can find joy in the Eternal, together!

> *Isa Upanishad* – 'Working thus, a man may wish for a life of a hundred years. Only actions done in God bind not the soul of man.'

This second paragraph of the Isa Upanishad connects directly with the Hebrew Scriptures in which the life of a human being is certainly described as finite and in which a life with God (the covenant and the relation with the Father) is what matters. However, the distinction needs to be made very clearly – for the Upanishads there is an ongoing cycle in which *dharma* as teaching and action creates the possibility of attaining the exit of *samsara* and *nirvana* as a state that is beyond human life and human suffering. For the Upanishads show less concern for good deeds but for a life beyond the material in which eternity is acquired within such a state. During eternity and in this state of existence time is not human, but time is a life with the Eternal in which the body does not matter; what matters is the interior mind that brings the unison of the OM and the life with the Absolute. The main action is the location of the body in meditation and the execution of the knowledge that comes from the Absolute (*brahman*). Good deeds are those done through the mind rather than through the body, and a long life, being material, is empty if it is not directed to the absolute principle of existence, that is *brahman*. The soul is bound to *brahman* because the *atman* is a manifestation of the Absolute, and therefore, regardless of a body and an honest human existence, the *atman* remains in *brahman*. A human existence is therefore a good one connected to the Absolute. I note that the caste system as a statement of identity by the Brahmanic schools to locate themselves at the centre of society was not yet developed. The Vedic rituals accessible to all at the time of the Upanishads (600–400 BCE) were changing due to the expansion of trade, the appearance of Hindu nobilities and their military expansion. What followed was social division, class and eventually the differentiation by caste.

> *Isa Upanishad* – 'There are demon-haunted worlds, regions
> of utter darkness. Whoever in life denies the Spirit falls into
> that darkness of death.'

This third paragraph allows for the possibility of dark worlds as opposed to worlds of light and fire provided by the morning and evening rituals of the Vedic priests. The Upanishads, as the end of the Vedas, introduce the absolute need to recognize knowledge of *brahman* as a state of being that will not allow darkness. States of rejection of the spiritual sense of the *atman* would bring the person into the dark world of demons, flesh-eating creatures that make human beings suffer. Death is not a biological consequence but a state of mind in which a human being rejects the possibility of the Spirit, of Light, of the brightness that comes in human life of the understanding of the Spirit, and of *brahman* as the unifying principle of absoluteness and spiritual awakening. The text brings the fears that the Hebrew Scriptures share in that there is darkness where there is no creation, and dangerous waters above and below the earth.

> *Isa Upanishad* – 'The Spirit, without moving, is swifter than the mind; the senses cannot reach him: He is ever beyond them. Standing still, he overtakes those who run. To the ocean of his being, the spirit of life leads the stream of actions.'

This fourth paragraph starts defining the infinite existence of *brahman*, beyond our understanding, and beyond our spatial temporality. All actions return to *brahman*, and all actions originate from *brahman* in a way that a human being who has knowledge becomes part of this absolute eternity, but *brahman* does not become part of our world of actions. There are challenges here to the Vedic priesthood, to actions as conditioning knowledge, and to knowledge as discoveries from personal knowledge. Everything comes and goes to *brahman*, who in turn does not change because of these material processes but provides the energy for actions that after all evolve from *brahman*. The lessons of this Upanishad are the possibilities of knowing by human beings as creatures but the non-importance of creation and non-creation, regardless of the principle of absoluteness that is present within all sentient beings.

The Spirit without moving opposes the Hebrew notion of Genesis, of the Spirit hovering over the water, but nevertheless triggers the action of creation at the beginning. Later, the Spirit would descend upon those chosen to lead the bridging between the divine and the human in the person of Jesus of Nazareth, and on the disciples, that are present at Pentecost from all nations and all languages of the earth. It is this notion of the Trinitarian Spirit, free and creative, that becomes a significant way of linking the Upanishads with the Christian notion of service, community and action, notions stressed by Bede Griffiths in all his engagements with an Indian Christianity. For, in the advanced thought of Griffiths, 'the gift of the Spirit which manifests the non-dual nature of the godhead, the human consciousness is raised to participation in the divine consciousness'.[26]

In my current eremitic situation, it is that Spirit that mediates the duality and non-duality of a Christian–Hindu dialogue. For it is the Spirit that is invoked to come and warm our hearts to God's humanity and to all those who follow a different ritual path within the same journey. Come Holy Spirit and renew the face of the earth! Spirit of God, warm our hearts to others, that we may be one! The human rational language that we use is changed by the Spirit and becomes a form of love for others in a mystical language that dwells in that silence, learning with the Spirit how to silently hover over the waters, with no judgement, no anger, no perception and no objective, only in love.

> *Isa Upanishad* – 'He moves, and he moves not. He is far, and he is near. He is within all, and he is outside all.'

This fifth paragraph reminds us of the great dilemmas of a language that is culturally constructed. We belong to a society and our education has given us an understanding of matter and spirit. This is correct, and there is no need for anger or despite towards a shared humanity that needs education, boundaries, purity and guidelines, and towards human beings who are happy within a way of life. However, the Upanishads as well as the Buddhist teaching of the *gate gate paragate* challenge our being by suggesting moving forward, moving beyond – in Christian terms, to move above. Why is it that most language metaphors use the language of builders and of limited spaces and human actions? The language of the Spirit is a language of love in which the human spirit moves beyond what we have learned in love. It is in love for other human beings whom God loves that I try to understand something different, and the language of non-contradiction and non-duality that arises is only an expression of the limitations that we experience trying to move closer to that divine world and divine language.

The issue of a selective and discriminatory language is already present in Mascaró's translation; a son of his time, one would say. However, the Spirit is neither masculine nor feminine, as the Trinity before the human understanding of our language exists from eternity and is not bound by human terms that come after the creation of this universe among many other universes. It is interesting, though I am not sure that I would agree with it completely, that Bede Griffiths understood the Spirit as feminine. In his later understanding after a severe stroke, he realized that he had missed the feminine side of a human being most of his life. In Griffiths' words: 'the world comes forth from the Father, the eternal Ground of Being, in his Word, the Cosmic Person (*purusha*)…but it is the Spirit who conceives these "ideas" in her maternal womb and brings them forth in creation'.[27]

This paragraph of the Upanishads brings the direct clash between languages in which Christianity is founded on premises of Greek and Roman ways of understanding the world and in which God has been predicated through a contextual language. If something is, then it cannot be perceived as not being. The non-duality that the Upanishads bring to the end of the Vedas bring that first impossibility of dialogue, because dialogue is conceived as a rational occupation in that I explain to the other what I believe and I decide rationally how far I can go, depending on my Christian formation regarding purity, understood as having a final objective – that is, my personal eternal salvation and life with God. We should be always conscious of this difficulty. However, in our unconscious, and we must remember that our beliefs are somehow non-rational and contradictory to others, we are no more or less rational than others. The issue of belonging in one or another tradition was the duality and non-duality that challenged the very existence of the Christian ashrams in India after Vatican II. The difficulty was not solved by further committee meetings but by the acceptance that a mystical language was the way of understanding the diversity of the divine manifestation within India. Thus, for Panikkar, for example, 'mystical discourse is a language that speaks and means something, even though this something is ineffable and can only be "captured" by a leap of "love"'.[28]

> *Isa Upanishad* – 'Who sees all beings in his own Self, and his own Self in all beings, loses all fear.'

This sixth paragraph provides the self-location for an openness to dialogue. The Self in the Upanishads does not only provide difference but sameness. It is in difference that we start our journey, learning how different we are. It is in the sameness of Self and surrounding evidence that we end, because in the journey we learn that after all we have lots in common. The Self does not fear any longer another human being who is very similar and with whom it can find traces of a shared humanity and a shared divinity. Thus, the Dalai Lama's common understanding that we are after all human beings and that we are born and then we die. What divides us in the middle of this process of human maturation disappears completely when we die, and the phenomenon of ceasing to breathe biologically is common to all human beings even for a few seconds. It is at that moment when eternal life and immortality would have to divide us once again. But at that moment God will make all things new, and those who have managed to exit *samsara* would have attained eternal bliss. Thus, the need I would argue for: an extended exploration by Christians and Hindus of the Upanishads and of an ongoing unconscious sense of togetherness in the facts of death. The moment of death brings human sorrow and grief to those who are left behind; it brings a change of materiality and existence to those who have died and have faced the possibilities of an eternal bliss.

In this chapter I have outlined some of the enormous possibilities of feeling togetherness between practitioners of different religious traditions by reading texts of more than one tradition in the spirit of meditation and prayer and as an act of love for the other. I would argue that it is only when we spend time with the other through symbols and prayers and by using a mystical language of love that we can grow into the understanding of the other. In fact, there is one common journey with different paths, in love and respect, with one common port of arrival: biological death. Thus in the following chapter I focus on issues of genocide and death as common human points of encounter by examining Pope Francis' visit to Auschwitz and his silence throughout the visit to this infamous extermination camp.

Chapter 6

THE SILENCE OF DEATH

Lord, have mercy on your people!
Lord, forgiveness for so much cruelty!

Pope Francis at Auschwitz, 29 July 2016[1]

On 29 July 2016 Pope Francis visited Auschwitz-Birkenau in the context of his visit to Poland.[2] Pope John Paul II and Benedict XVI also visited the extermination camps during their pontificates. Indeed, John Paul II visited Auschwitz several times before becoming pope in order to visit the cell where St Maximilian Kolbe had died.[3] Benedict XVI accompanied John Paul II on that day in June 1979 as archbishop of Munich-Freising and later visited Auschwitz as pope, being aware that he visited as 'a son of the German people'.[4] A man of reason, Benedict XVI spoke of God in the following terms: 'The God in whom we believe is a God of reason – a reason, to be sure, which is not a kind of cold mathematics of the universe, but is one with love and with goodness.'[5] Pope Francis' visit was somehow different because silence was the norm of his visit. His visit reminded me of my own memories of captivity at the Villa Grimaldi (Chile) that I have outlined elsewhere and my first return to the torture camp in silence.[6] The silence that Pope Francis brought to the memory of the Shoah was highlighted by his pursuing of two eremitic actions: he sat silently at the entrance of Auschwitz on a chair for what seemed an endless time, and later he sat in darkness and in silence in the cell where Maximilian Kolbe, a priest who gave his life for another human being, was kept before his execution. Death and silence go always together, and death remains a moment of profound definition for the rest of humanity, particularly in unjust and cruel circumstances.[7]

In this final chapter I explore the ethical imperative of being in silence for others, another characteristic of the way of a hermit and of inter-religious dialogue in places where followers of the world religions suffered and were annihilated. This silent recognition of the suffering of many, a majority of them Jews, who died in Auschwitz, was a public recognition by Pope Francis of the common journey that all followers of the world religions can pursue by assuming that all religious communities and all human beings at one point or another have been violently attacked and killed by others. They share a history and they share a journey if they decide to accept this human commonality. It is within such silence that peace and understanding in a common journey can challenge any message of hatred and violence towards others. It is, I would argue, the contribution of a hermit to maintain such spiritual solidarity regardless of the ups and downs of dialogue in general, and particularly of interfaith dialogue.

HERMENEUTICS
THE HERMENEUTICS OF SILENCE

The interpretation of silence as a moment in time and space reminds us that silence is a creative moment for the self and for the context in which such silence takes place. It is not only the physical silence that can be created but the silence of the soul, the silence of the heart and ultimately the silence of the self. The first step of a hermit as outlined in the first part of this work is to sit in a cell and wait for God. The interpretation of such silent movement recreates three spheres of understanding that provide in turn three layers in which silence becomes the link between the first level of the individual self, the second level of a personal transformation and the third level of existence within a cosmic world. It is in that cosmic world beyond humanity in which silence reigns that silence becomes a song, a rainbow, a cosmic canticle. If silence can be interpreted as the creative and meaningful link between the first and the third levels, death becomes within the second level the means to an end, the maturation of the self to enter the cosmic realm of existence. Thus to interpret silence in all its creativity and to experience such silence requires the silencing of the word in order to focus on what comes before the word which is silence.[8] For Raimon Panikkar, for example, the expression 'In the beginning was the Word' is not a claim that the Word is the beginning. Rather, 'the Beginning is Silence, the Void, Non-Being, the Abyss, Darkness, or other symbols in many other traditions'.[9] The Word is not silent, and it is not silence, Panikkar argues, but 'the true word emerges from the silence, "shattering" it, going beyond it, overcoming it' so that 'silence doesn't speak, it says nothing, but it makes the saying possible; silence inspires it, since it dwells there'.[10] It is in silence that reality is united, because 'silence is one, words are many'.[11]

It is this possibility of silence as a creative communal moment before the word is spoken that Pope Francis emphasized in his conscious wish not to speak at Auschwitz but to remain silent. He had expressed the wish in the following words: 'I would like to go to that place of horror without speeches, without crowds – only the few people necessary,' he explained. 'Alone, enter, pray. And may the Lord give me the grace to cry.'[12] 'Memoria e silenzio' (memory and silence) was the headline of *L'Osservatore Romano*, the daily Vatican newspaper in the edition that reported the visit one day later.[13]

THE HERMENEUTICS OF DEATH

It was through moments of silence, extended ones for any papal visit, that Francis tried to comprehend death at Auschwitz.[14] He arrived by car at the entrance to the museum and then walked on his own through the main gates, slowly into the camp, as many had entered during the extermination of 1.1 million people, the majority of them Jews. The camp had been established in 1940, built around the city of Oświęcim, as Polish prisoners taken after the Nazi invasion of Poland increased in numbers.[15] Once inside the camp, he sat on a chair in Roll Call Square for a period of time reflecting and praying, trying not to be disturbed by the Vatican photographer or the security that kept a watchful eye on those passing by. At the end of this period in silence Pope Francis kissed one of the wooden pillars and departed for the wall at which prisoners were executed, a wall destroyed by the camp guards (1943) and rebuilt by prisoners in 1946. Another long moment of silence took place at the cell where Fr Maximilian Kolbe (1894–1941) died, now a publicly proclaimed saint for the Catholic Church.

Fr Kolbe had made the ultimate sacrifice willingly at a time when a Polish man was going to be sent to the block where prisoners were starved to death. It was the order of the commandant of Auschwitz that for every escapee ten prisoners were to be sent to the starvation block, where they died of hunger and thirst. On one of those occasions when ten prisoners had been chosen, a Polish man cried, wondering what would happen to his wife and children. Fr Kolbe stepped forward, identified himself to the camp commander as a Catholic priest and asked that he might be sent to the starvation block instead of the man who cried. Kolbe argued that he didn't have a family and that the man had a family to return to. The commander agreed to the request, and Kolbe was sent to the starvation block where two weeks later he was given a lethal injection as he was one of the last prisoners left to die. His body was burnt with many other bodies.[16]

Pope Francis remained in silence within the dark cell and later signed the book of honour with the words 'Lord, have mercy on your people, Lord, forgiveness for so much cruelty' (Franciscus 29.7.2016). The silence of such poignant moments was then changed for an emotional meeting with some of the camp survivors who showed him photos and with whom he embraced. And then he departed for Birkenau, an extension of the Auschwitz camp.

MEETING WITH THE RIGHTEOUS ONES

Pope Francis visited and prayed at the Monument to the Victim of the Nations, inaugurated in 1967 between Crematoria II and III. There is a phrase written on the tombstones in the 23 languages spoken by prisoners: 'For ever let this place be a cry of despair and a warning to humanity, where the Nazis murdered about one and a half million men, women and children, mainly Jews, from various countries of Europe. Auschwitz-Birkenau 1940–1945.' Pope Francis prayed in silence and lit a candle with 1000 people in attendance. He met 25 'Righteous among the Nations', that is, non-Jews who saved Jews from Nazi persecution. After that meeting a rabbi recited Psalm 130 in Hebrew, a text that was read in Polish by one of the survivors.

The presence of the 'Righteous' provides a reflection on the possibility of goodness and a common journey. For in the midst of any horror there are choices, and some of those choices are to aid even those who are not one's own people. Thus, in the preface to the diary of Carl Schrade, a Swiss national who spent 11 years in different Nazi concentration camps, Fabrice d'Almeida argues that 'regardless of circumstances or duties there is always the possibility of behaving as a human being and of preserving the highest sentiments of human nature' (my translation).[17] Yad Vashem, the World Holocaust Remembrance Center, outlines the 'Righteous' as follows:

> They were ordinary human beings, and it is precisely their humanity that touches us and should serve as a model. So far Yad Vashem has recognized 'Righteous' from 44 countries and nationalities; there are Christians from all denominations and churches, Muslims and agnostics; men

and women of all ages; they come from all walks of life; highly educated people as well as illiterate peasants; public figures as well as people from society's margins; city dwellers and farmers from the remotest corners of Europe; university professors, teachers, physicians, clergy, nuns, diplomats, simple workers, servants, resistance fighters, policemen, peasants, fishermen, a zoo director, a circus owner, and many more.[18]

It is the possibility of acting ethically regardless of being caught and in danger of death that makes a human being honest and good. The silence of complicity has been invoked for too long as the only possible response in a time of mass killings. However, those honest and ethical responses to a very serious historical period come out of a life of small responses by witnesses to suffering, and of a personal prayer that brings the response to the Gospel and to life as clearly opposed to the silence of complicity in the face of death. Today, and in our contemporary context, I think that when homosexuals or transsexuals have been killed in homophobic attacks, all of us who didn't challenge somebody who made a trivial homophobic remark are accomplices. Jokes and remarks against Jews today foreshadow a violent act that can be stopped when the initial remark has been uttered in a bar, at a dinner or in a corridor.

It is the possibility of silence that allows us to know about those who died, particularly those who died at the Shoah for being ethnically Jewish and whose descendants live among us today. The ethical responsibility of not forgetting them is not only a Jewish duty but also a Christian duty: to remember all those human beings who died unjustly under machineries of extermination and hate. We are all human beings on a journey, and the silence of Pope Francis allowed for a very public sign that spoke to us about the meaningful silence of a suffering common humanity.

SILENCES AND DEATHS
SILENCES

The noise of youth singing in the early hours, and I return with Pope Francis to the camps, the concentration camps of humanity and towards my own camp. 2.50am and the first silence of the morning arises at Nalanda, while the three budgies that accompany my prayer do not know if to sleep or to arise. It is at this moment of the night or of the day that my prayer goes to the memory of those who died in Auschwitz, and to those who survived Auschwitz and had to deal with the death of their relatives, the absence of their lovers and sometimes the absence of God. I cannot sleep in those mornings because the *zikkaron* (memory) of the Jews killed brings back my own dead and my own memories. The memory of the dead brings the possibility that they are not killed a second time, as suggested by Elie Wiesel, a Jewish survivor of Auschwitz. For Wiesel, today's look at the past is as important as the past itself.[19]

It is in those mornings that I pray with the dead, those who have gone to the Sheol, to the place of the dead, and who have been beside me since those years at my own camp. The silence of years allowed me to feel the complicity of those who died, but nobody was to know. Only my grandfather knew, the righteous one; in his own sorrow for his son's death he covered me with righteousness and love – he was for me the Righteous One. How I miss those who died because they were part of my life, of my journey, and I could never return to them. I was the one who survived in silence in order to survive the social death that the secrets of the dead could not tell. Why was it that I was a member of the only family in Chile who having had a relative executed didn't spit on the military for the killing? Why was it that they feared losing their jobs and their existence while others lost their lives? Why was it that even when the memory of

Marcella at the Villa Grimaldi was celebrated in 2009, my family treated it with silence?

Part of the hermit's life is to be with the living in prayer and to be with the dead in silence.

The hermit, as I have experienced, is a bridge between those who fear and those who do not fear any longer because they are dead. I do not fear the dead because they have passed through the threshold of mystery and they have survived the ordeal. And within such experience nobody understands any longer. Thus I understand the experience of Pope Francis in silence. It is the courageous experience of not saying that we can understand evil or death; we cannot, because we are alive, not dead, and we have not experienced the ultimate passage, that is, death. The voices of the dead accompany the hermitage prayer, and in lighting a candle for the dead I pray for their families.

> May they find peace! May they enjoy life! May they be respected! Be they Jews, Christians, Muslims, Hindus or Buddhists, may they find their path which has become my own path. May I be a bridge for them through prayer, may I love them, may I respect them so that never again human beings be killed in the name of religion, because any path of ritual and metaphysics is sacred, good and loving. May I know them better by reading their memoirs and testimonies.[20] My own memory is a silent memory.[21] It was dark and grey at the Cuartel Terranova. I was kept outside in June, and it was cold. I didn't shower or brush my teeth and I was in silence. The noises of people moving and of prisoners in silence was at times changed by shouts, screams and the odour of electricity in the night. The odour of burning skin in the night, of sparks and blood, and urine and filth. Barbecued flesh, empty sockets, crushed legs, and silence. When I see my forehead and the deep line of cut metal on it, I know it happened. When I see my twisted collar bone after showering, I know it happened.

Human beings with ideals and dreams were crushed by their interrogators until they could only howl like animals, until they expired their last. Then they were taken in lorries to the port, put onto boats and thrown into the sea. They stayed there in silence until the silence without democracy ended, and there were memories and pain and more silence in case memories could challenge the arrival of democracy. I was spared, provided I kept silent. I did for 25 years until my visit to the camp and my writings started in earnest.[22]

The inspiration from Elie Wiesel, camp survivor and 1986 Nobel Prize winner, comes at a moment in which it seems that memories are forgotten and less important if those memories are not catalysed by one single individual and his silence. For it is the individual that embodies the universe with its memories, as in the Talmudic use of a sentence to engrave Oskar Schindler's ring so that 'he who saves one life saves the universe entire'. Thus, the responsibility of one person's memory becomes the universal memory of a period in which millions were killed but only the experience of one could be embraced. And, like Pope Francis in his visit to Auschwitz, Elie Wiesel needs silence to actualize the memory of millions: 'Writing becomes more difficult, more exhausting, more pressing. I need solitude. Silence.'[23] For the memories of silence could be erased, as proven by my search for Elie Wiesel's books in every bookshop in Santiago during July 2016, with the result that it was impossible to find any. Those books were prohibited most probably by the military censor in 1986. During that year Wiesel received the Nobel Peace Prize. The military regime had to face the recognition of a Jew as a notable person in a year in which Wole Soyinka won the Nobel Prize for Literature, being an African, a Nigerian and a black person.

The silence of a hermit, as it must be becoming clearer, embraces the possibilities of humanity in relation to God. Through silence the hermit follows a path which in daily materiality provides a discipline, a structured daily life that can discipline the body, an accomplice of the possibility of forgetting others through self-care. For to forget God is to forget the actual materiality of God in the world through a human medium. It is through a person that God acts in the world, and the person's actions are metaphysical as far as the movement that comes through action is activated through prayer. Thus, an activity of the soul in Christianity makes things happen if those happenings have a good-natured causation. Silence does originally provide the realization of the ills of death as a life without a metaphysical aspiration and realm of action. However, such silence continues quieting the body until silence becomes the message, and the message an action towards life. I am reminded here once again of the good actions (*karma*) whose fruits can be transferred to others. I can pray in silence for other sentient beings to send good energies that in turn would create good intentions, and that in turn can create good actions. In fact, the virtual reality that seems to dominate contemporary life whereby we talk to somebody else who is not physically present is nevertheless present within the lay vow of a bodhisattva. If the ordinary vow to achieve nirvana is a material one because it involves body and speech, 'the Bodhisattva vow, being born from mind (and essentially a matter of one's aspiration), is non-material; it continues into the next rebirth and persists if the thought that bears it does not fail'.[24]

DEATHS

It is at the end of a biological life that the enormous difference of understanding within peoples will be realized. At that moment, those who suggest that nothing happens after death, meaning there is no continuation of life as we know it, and those who are quite certain about what will happen, will face (maybe) a divine surprise. The notion of God, the Absolute, nothingness or reincarnation is permeated by our belief and, while I recognize the Christian creeds, I await being surprised by a God who is bigger than our limited understanding. Regardless of whatever happens within individual judgements or a universal judgement, all these events are certainly beyond our control and our agency. Grace is a gift from God, and the decision of who will receive the ultimate grace of being with God for eternity will not depend on any of us. We are all human beings, and as human beings we recognize the absolute and infinite agency of God over our material world. However, the moment of biological death, and therefore the moment of death, becomes a central moment for our human journey, and the eremitic vocation accompanies human beings and indeed sentient beings until that moment. The journey towards death within life requires a virtual connection of love and prayer that challenges the somehow selfish position of 'my way' to eternal life or the intellectual position of self-understanding in which I can feel better if I pray.

It is the phenomenon of death that traditionally has united the possibilities of a common journey between Christians and Hindus, and it is to the experience of a journey towards death that we must return. A *sadhu* told me that it is through death that we attain immortality and that it is through a common search for wisdom and understanding that we could become united on the road. For, 'if you think "I know well", little truth you know'.[25] Thus, the Katha Upanishad provides a dialogue between Death and Nachiketas in which Nachiketas reminds Death about 'that sacred fire which leads to heaven'.[26] Death's response to such an allusion was as follows: 'that fire which is the means of attaining the infinite worlds, and is also their foundation, is hidden in the sacred place of the heart'.[27]

DEATH AND DIALOGUE

It was a remarkable expression of infinite togetherness that when Ramesh Babu, a Hindu from Amritsar, came to Scotland with Kabir Babu to sign the St Andrews Declaration for a Shared Humanity in September 2016, he had time to visit my hermitage.

During that short visit, we had time to talk about the life of the hermit and the feelings and prayers that arise within the small hours of the night and of the morning. Ramesh told me about a night when he couldn't sleep and wrote a poem about death, because in between snoozing and awakening he didn't know if he was alive or dead any longer. We were having tea and scones in a hotel in Anstruther, and the normality of death and the conversation about death was clearly shown within this moment of conversation. Ramesh asked Kabir to read me the poem aloud, the poem entitled 'The Night of the Dead', and so Kabir read:

I lost my father, lost my riches, I lost myself… I died.
There is a land of the dead,
Silent and forgotten…
I remember how I quietly took my first step into this world,
Letting go of my mother's wail I galloped
    from childhood to manhood,
From learning to earning,
From being to becoming.
The dead smile vacantly into the emptiness,
They don't blink, they don't question,
They move as moved…heavy and forlorn.
This one fateful night haunts me,
Which is why I am writing to you.
I was sitting in my chair that night
    when I was screamed to life!
I had to hear that I was alive still, breathing they said.
I pled, I told them I was not alive, neither was
    I a crook but they did not give in.
I was forced onto my feet, I had to swear on
    all my Gods that I wasn't living,
I was among the dead and I wasn't a crook.
Nowadays, I lie in my grave rotten and
    spent, being gnawed by insects.
I have befriended my gnawers and contemplate… I
    have sworn on all my Gods, am I really dead?[28]

The exchanges about the dead and about death were not terrifying but reassuring because the exchange between us was that of three people who took for granted that one day, as will happen to every human being, we will die. Tea and scones with such a conversation could be unsettling for Western habits; however, I remind the reader that within a morning Buddhist *puja* (prayers) tea, bread and jam are served, challenging some of our Western notions that you cannot eat while you pray. In fact, those who celebrate the Eucharist do, as bread and wine are shared while prayers are taking place. Dichotomies between life and death seem natural, but it is our mind that has learned through social habits to differentiate moments of prayer (of purity) and moments of feeding (impurity). The boundaries between these two moments are less accentuated in Asia, and the rhythm of human beings who utter opinions about the metaphysical world is not left to philosophers or holy people but to human beings in their daily interaction. On this occasion, it made absolute sense to share some tea and have a conversation about Christian and Hindu realities, including death.

Thus the communion between the living and the dead, rightly proclaimed within the Christian creeds and actualized daily, for example in African life through libations, does not perturb their lives, but it can enrich them. The rich possibility to empathize with the dead and to visit the places where the dead died or are buried allows us to explore a clear commonality between Christians and Hindus: the moment of death. As the earth is moved or the funerary pyre fed with wood, we are reminded that this is the moment when our human agency ceases and where the divine agency takes complete control. We share this moment and this conviction and in sorrow we pause in prayer, accompanying those being buried or cremated because it is in that moment of death that a human being acquires, to paraphrase a Hindu, 'immortality', meaning the person cannot die again. That person will be born again for Hindus and will attain an eternal reward for Christians.

Within such experience of the dead and the burning or the burying of the dead, we can also find a way in which to pray for the dead of other religious traditions, indeed for all the dead, because in taking care of the dead we are taking care of the living. Thus the reflection by Elie Wiesel that 'those who utter funerary prayers do not usually say them for the dead but for the living, to console them, to pacify their spirit'.[29]

CONCLUSIONS: WITNESS TO DEATH, WITNESS TO SILENCE

The hermit is a witness to the daily meeting between the material world and the metaphysical longing for completion, for peace, for love. By living under a discipline of life, the hermit witnesses to the enormous possibilities of a journey with God in silence, a journey with others in love, a journey of witness to death and suffering in which, as during the moment of death, there is always love, triumph and laughter after witnessing to death. A witness to death and resurrection, the hermit sits in his hermitage and waits for God. However, the hermit sits waiting accompanied by the memory of many others who have experienced solitude and suffering because those witnesses to persecution and death have joined Jesus of Nazareth, a prisoner sentenced to death for proclaiming his own relationship of love with the Father. Thus, the hermit sits on his own, but the moment that God arrives, God does not come alone but the God of many and of All comes surrounded by history and with the history of a whole humanity. By accepting the search for God and love of neighbour, the Christian hermit accepts the challenge to love deeper and to bring grace to others through silence and prayer. The hermit becomes a witness of human and divine history and a witness to the God who loves all humanity but takes special care of the poor and the marginalized among those millions of fellow pilgrims.

I recall here the example given by Elie Wiesel, who in his classic work *Night* introduced the memory of those who died and the memory of those who are suffering because of other human beings' selfishness as an ethical project and a personal one. Thus, in his Nobel Prize acceptance speech, he argued that 'if we forget, we are guilty, we are accomplices'.[30] For someone who had been forced to be a 'guest' at Auschwitz and Buchenwald, it is clear that 'our lives no longer belong to us alone; they belong to all those who need us desperately'.[31]

Within this human belonging in which we are all first and foremost human beings, there is a special relationship within the journey with those who follow a religious discipline or a philosophical system that brings them to bridge the material and the supra-natural. A life of ascetic endeavour and constant prayer is not only common to Christianity and Hinduism but arises out of a metaphysical commonality of the so-called world religions. Out of this commonality arises a natural and strong connection between the hermit and other traditions' hermits, and between the Christian hermit and all those who pray and meditate daily within Hinduism and Buddhism. Together, at a distance, and together in the same space, praying a silent common prayer and studying each other's texts can become a clear vehicle of a eremitic life dedicated to the virtual encouragement of others, particularly those who suffer, and the encouragement of others within and without one's religious traditions through interfaith dialogue. Prayer remains at the centre of this common venture, and welcoming members of other faiths to pray in silence together is a clear way forward. It was a meaningful practice during the conference that followed the signing of the St Andrews Declaration for a Shared Humanity in September 2016, and it is a way of praying together that Pope Francis has used to pray together in silence with Orthodox leaders and people of other languages and other traditions.

The hermit facilitates such encounters and goes to meet those who want to pray together in neutral places where purity and respect can be re-emphasized. A kind and encouraging word will always be part of the extension of the personal cell by bringing the Peace of God to others without trying to find solutions to ritual or intellectual diversities but by reaffirming the possibility that all religions and indeed all human beings can co-exist together.

To conclude these theological reflections on the way of the hermit today, I refer to one of the contributions by Pope Francis to contemporary Christian life, the encyclical *Laudato si'*, in which he reflects on the care of our planet, the common purpose we share to care for our common home.[32] The commonality between Christians and Hindus is outlined and reaffirmed when Francis reminds us that we are as human beings made of earth and that our body is made of the planet's elements, its air is what gives us breath and its water gives us life while restoring our energies.[33] Francis, following the practice by John XXIII, addressed this encyclical to all human beings who inhabit the same planet in the same way as John had spoken of the value of peace to all human beings who cared to listen to him.[34] The ecological crisis was also addressed in 1971 by Paul VI as a crisis of all human beings as well as within his address to the United Nations' agency for food (FAO) in the previous year.[35] John Paul II addressed all humanity when he called for a 'ecological global conversion' and for the development of an 'authentic human ecology'.[36] Benedict XVI followed this universal discussion by suggesting that every human being is not only 'spirit and will' but also 'nature'.[37] Thus Pope Francis followed a tradition of stressing the value of our care for the planet, particularly by those who profess faith or belong to a philosophical and symbolic system such as Hinduism.

While the Pope's contribution on ecological issues could be associated with a specific topic, these thoughts for the care of the planet recognize that other Christian churches and other religions have made significant contributions to these reflections.[38] I note here that Francis acknowledges the contribution of the Ecumenical Patriarch Bartholomew who has consistently argued that any crime against the planet is a crime against ourselves and a sin against God.[39] Bartholomew argues that Christians are called 'to accept the world as sacrament of communion, as a way of sharing with God and with one another at a global scale'.[40] Following from this contemporary Orthodox contribution, Francis, recognizing that the majority of humanity can be considered believers, argues for a dialogue between religions concerning the care of nature, the defence of the poor, and the construction of networks of respect and fraternity.[41]

The role and social position of the hermit as a liminal, non-partisan figure within religious structures of power, contested histories and divisive symbolic understandings remains a privileged one, because it helps to mediate conversations between the divine and the human, between different religious traditions and between different Christian traditions separated by theological understandings and political misunderstandings. It is my prayer, my wish and my desire that, following the example of the pioneer Christian *sadhus* of India, one day soon we 'may all be one', not because we can finally solve our human differences about the divine but because by coming closer to the divine we could accept that God is larger and more loving than all our differences. Let us embrace each other even with fear and let us prostrate ourselves in silent prayer together. Then we shall become sons and daughters of God. This is not a dream, this is our reality today, as it was for the Indian poet Kabir: 'Kabir says, renounce all family, caste, and clan. Turn into an ant, instead – pick the sugar from the sand and eat.'[42]

An Indian
Eucharistic Prayer[1]

Celebrant

O Supreme Lord of the Universe,
You fill and sustain everything around us
You turned, with the touch of your hand,
Chaos into order, darkness into light.
Unknown energies you hid in the heart of matter.
From you bursts forth the splendour of the sun
And the mild radiance of the moon.
Stars and planets without number
You set in ordered movement.
You are the source of the fire's heat and the wind's might,
Of the water's coolness and the earth's stability.
Deep and wonderful, the mysteries of your creation.

Congregation

We adore you, who are beyond all form!
You give form to everything, Lord of all creation!
We praise you, we thank you, we proclaim your glory!

Celebrant

God of all that lives,
Through countless ages
You have peopled the seas and rivers,
The mountains and plains,
With beings innumerable.

With power from you
The seed buds forth in blossom,
The tender shoot grows into a mighty tree,
Bird and beast multiply and fill the earth.
You are the life of all that lives.

Congregation
We adore you, O source of life!
All creatures look to you, Lord of power!
We praise you, we thank you, we proclaim your glory!

Celebrant
God of all salvation,
You formed people in your own image.
You created them male and female,
You willed their union and harmony
You entrusted the earth to their care
And promised your blessing to all their descendants.
You gave them the spirit of discernment to know you,
The power of speech to celebrate your glory,
The strength of love to give themselves in joy to you.
In this wondrous way, O God,
You called them to share
In your being,
Your own knowledge,
Your own bliss.

Congregation
We adore you, O lover of all!
In you is the source of our life.
We praise you, we thank you, we proclaim your glory!

Celebrant

Lord of all ages,
Father most kind and merciful,
You want all people to reach the shores of salvation.
Even when they fail to respond to your call,
You do not abandon them to themselves.
In your unchanging fidelity
You wish your love for them
To stand forever.
Your covenant with Noah shows your providence
Through the constant cycles of nature.
In the tempest of Job's affliction,
You revealed the mystery of human life.
You chose Melchisedech
A priest from among the nations,
To bless Abraham your servant.

Congregation

We adore you, Lord of all ages!
You are ever at work to shape the destinies of human beings,
We praise you, we thank you, we proclaim your glory!

Celebrant

God of the nations,
You are the desire and hope
Of all who search for you with a sincere heart
You are the Power of the almighty
Adored as Presence hidden in nature.
You reveal yourself
To the seers in their quest for knowledge,
To devout who seek you through sacrifice and detachment,
To every person approaching you by the path of love,
You enlighten the hearts that long for release
By conquest of desire and universal kindness.
You show mercy to those who submit
To your inscrutable decrees.

Congregation

We adore you, light divine!
You shine bright in the hearts of those who seek you.
We praise you, we thank you, we proclaim your glory!

Celebrant

God of the covenant,
In your gracious love for all people
You called Abraham
To be the father of a great nation.
Through Moses your servant
You gathered your scattered children into a people.
Despite their infidelity,
You never failed to speak to them through the Prophets
And to save them through your mighty deeds.
You instilled into their hearts an eager hope
For that awaited day of the Saviour to come,
The day of peace and favour for all.

Congregation

We adore you, God of promise!
Your erring people you pursue with love.
We praise you, we thank you, we proclaim your glory!

Celebrant

O God invisible,
At the favourable time
You were pleased to become visible to us.
Your Word, your only-begotten Son,
Took on our human condition
And was born of the Virgin Mary.
As Supreme Teacher and Master,
He imparted the words of eternal life
To the poor and humble of heart,
And went about doing good.
When his hour had come,

Of his own accord he laid down his life
As sacrifice for our sins.
Raised from the dead by you, Father,
He became for us the source of life
And sent the Holy Spirit
To fill the world with you and peace.

Now we pray you, Father,
Send this same Spirit
To fill these gifts of bread and wine
With his divine power,
And to make present among us
The great mystery of our salvation.

Congregation
Come, O Spirit Supreme,
Come, O Spirit all holy,
Come, O Spirit who fill the universe.

Celebrant
At the supper
Which he longed to share with his disciples,
Your Son, Jesus Christ,
Showed the depth of his love,
Though Lord and Master,
He did the humble work of a slave
By washing their feet.
During the meal
He took bread in his sacred hands,
Gave you praise and thanks,
Broke the bread and gave it to his disciples, saying:

Take this, all of you, and eat it:
This is my body which will be given up for you.
Do this to celebrate the memorial of me.

Congregation
Amen.

Celebrant

In the same way after supper,
He took the cup.
Again he gave you praise and thanks,
Gave the cup to his disciples, saying:

Take this, all of you, and drink from it:
This is the cup of my blood,
The blood of the new and everlasting covenant.
It will be shed for you and for all
So that sins may be forgiven.
Do this to celebrate the memorial of me.

Congregation

Amen.

Celebrant

And so, Father,
In gratitude we celebrate the memorial
Of the obedient death of your son,
Of his glorious resurrection from the dead,
His triumphant ascension into heaven
And his outpouring of the Spirit in whom the Church is born.
While in glory he intercedes for us
    before your throne of mercy,
We on earth await his return.
When he comes, he will gather up the fruits of redemption
Hold them together in his fullness
And place them at your feet.
United with him in this mystery of salvation,
We offer you
His unique and holy sacrifice.

Congregation

We announce your death
And proclaim your resurrection, Lord Jesus;
Gather all your people into your kingdom
When you come in glory.

Celebrant

Merciful Father,
Bring together all your people in the Holy Spirit,
Help them live in unity and fellowship
With Francis our Pope,
.... our bishop,
The patriarchs and pastors of all Churches.

We pray you, Father,
Crown the yearnings of this our ancient land
With the knowledge and love of your Son.
Bless the efforts of all those who labour
To build our country into a nation
Where the poor and the hungry will have their fill,
Where all people will live in harmony,
Where justice and peace, unity and love will reign.
Bless also all our brethren
Who are not present at this Eucharist.

Grant to our departed brothers and sisters
And all who longed for you
A share in your bliss.
Welcome them into your Kingdom,
Where Mary the Virgin Mother of God,
The saints of all lands and ages,
St Thomas, St Francis Xavier and St N...
Unceasingly pray for us
And help us to share in the riches,
Of your Son, Our Lord Jesus Christ.

Loving Father,
Send down your Spirit,
The fullness of your bliss,
To fill with joy and peace
All of us who share
In the Body and Blood of Christ,
That we may be one in Him,

And manifest our unity
In loving service.
May he be the pledge of our resurrection
And lead us in hope to the shore of eternal life
With all the just in the Kingdom of Heaven.

Congregation
Supreme Spirit, Spirit Divine,
Awaken us to your loving presence.

Celebrant
In the Oneness of the Supreme Spirit
Through Christ who unites all things in his fullness
We and the whole creation give to you,
God of all, Father of all,
Honour and glory, thanks and praise,
Worship and adoration,
Now and in every age,
For ever and ever.

Congregation
Amen. You are the fullness of reality,
One without a second,
Being, knowledge, bliss!
OM, TAT, SAT!

The Great Amen of humanity, nature and the cosmos opens the way of the great interfaith Amen of Christians and Hindus in which the post-colonial God, without the power of human empires and nations in strife, brings the possibility of unity in joy, peace and a road together.

A Christian–Hindu
Morning Prayer

The prostration on the floor is at the start of this morning prayer.

Then there is silence while those who are praying sit on the floor after having greeted the sun and the light of the morning, symbols of the Risen Christ and of the presence of Hindus within their ritual prayers to the sun in India and beside the home altars throughout the world.

> *I sit on the floor aware of the light.*
> *I sit on the floor aware of my Hindu brothers and sisters.*
> *I sit on the floor greeting the morning and the Lord!*
> *Let the hymns to Christ and to Shiva resound!*
> *Let the Amen and the OM resound together!*
> *Let the sun shine on Christians and Hindus!*
> *Let the Peace that surpasses all understanding reign!*
> *Let visions of the Ganges and of Jerusalem shine upon us!*
> *Amen. OM TAT TA.*[1]

This prayer is followed by the recitation of one of the Upanishads.

> *Amen. OM TAT TA.*

CHRISTIAN–HINDU EVENING PRAYERS[1]

EVENING PRAYER 1

The evening prayer starts when all are sitting on the floor and a candle has been lit. The candle is surrounded by flowers with a cup of water beside it.

The evening prayer begins with some minutes of silence to remember one's faults and the faults of humanity that have today created injustice, anger, despair, discrimination and violence.

The minutes in silence are followed by the chanting of the Amen and the OM.

*Trinity of Light and Fire, within the darkness
    the light arises as an image of the Lord.
It is evening, and darkness is already upon us, a
    darkness that only You can enter and remove.*
Amen.
*We give thanks for this day, for those whom we have
    encountered and who have given us joy and
    peace as well as those who have tried our feelings
    and thoughts. May they have peace tonight!*
Amen.
*Lord of all bliss, we sit in communion with our fellow
    human beings who are praying and chanting at
    the banks of the river Ganges, of Mama Ganga,
    those who are witnessing the fire ceremony.*
OM.

Give peace and light to those who have left the
ashes of their loved ones at the river.
May they find peace and their loved ones
an exit from suffering and pain.
OM.

Reading of the Isa Upanishad.

Reading of Psalm 90.

Father of Light, Lord of the Universe, we pray for
the widows and orphans, for those who are
hungry, for those who have lost hope, for the ill
and infirm, for those despised by society, may
we send them our prayers and your light.

Water is sprinkled with the fingers on the flowers and those present.

Peace and bliss! OM TAT TA. Amen.

The prayer ends with some minutes of silence.

EVENING PRAYER 2

Candles are lit in communion with the fires at Varanasi.

Lord, come to our aid.
Lord, do not leave us.
Blessed is the name of the Lord!
Who made heaven and earth!
Blessed are the names of the Lord!
Everywhere, anywhere, and nowhere.

[silence and meditation]

Tonight we beseech the Spirit,
as to help us visualize the beyond.
Beyond our small location, beyond our selfishness

Towards humanity, all those who are like us
Who trust and fear, laugh and cry in a day.

Tonight we beseech the Spirit beside the Ganges
With the pilgrims who are chanting beside the fires
Let us Lord visualize them, let us be with them
Protect them Lord in their evening
Bless them with your Spirit together with their families.

Tonight we beseech the Spirit in the gats[2]
May those who mourn their loss
Find joy, peace and immortality
May they find the sound beyond every sound
OM TAT SAT!

Tonight we beseech the Spirit at the fires
Lord protect the weak, the infirm, the poor
May they find consolation and justice
May they teach us the beyond of any Name
May they give us your words and silence.

Lord of many names be with us
As the silence of the night makes us strong
In your presence of immortality
Protect us as we sleep, as we pray in dreams
May you protect us Christians and Hindus, your children!

[silence and meditation]

Recitation of Psalm 90.

> *OM. This eternal Word is all: what was, what is and what*
> *shall be, and what beyond is in eternity. All is OM.*
> *The word OM as one sound is the fourth state of*
> *supreme consciousness. It is beyond the senses and*
> *is the end of evolution. It is non-duality and love.*
> *He goes with his self to the supreme Self who knows*
> *this, who knows this. (Mandukya Upanishad)*
> *Amen. OM TAT SAT.[3]*

ROMAN INDIAN LITURGY (EUCHARIST)

The Eucharist starts in silence with everybody sitting on the floor.

A moment of silence follows, requesting pardon for the sins of those present and the social injustices of the contemporary world.

> *Lord of all times and all universes*
> *Come to us today with your bliss*
> *Sustain us in our thanksgiving*
> *Make us holy through renunciation.*
> *Amen. OM TAT TA.*

First reading: The Isa Upanishad.

Chanting of the OM.

Second reading: Gospel of John 1.1–14.

A period of silence follows.

Offertory – as it was done at Shantivanam: 'the preparation of bread and wine at the offertory is embellished by the "sacrifice of the elements" – water, earth (flowers), air (incense), and fire, as in the Hindu rites of puja'.[1] The elements are acknowledged on the altar with the water being sprinkled on the elements with the tips of the fingers, the flowers and the air being sanctified with the fire. The flower symbolizes the ultimate divinity – that divinity that one tries to reach: 'the flower floats in the middle of the primordial waters, drifting from shore to shore…it has no roots in this world'.[2] That fire could be a match, a bowl with a candle in, or even a candle that is lifted and moved around the elements with piety and veneration. It is at that moment that the unity takes place with those Hindus who are performing the fire ceremony, with Buddhists who are burning candles to the Lord Buddha in their temples, with Christians all over the world, and indeed with the whole of humanity.

Celebrant: In the Oneness of the Supreme Spirit through Christ who unites all things in his fullness we and the whole creation give to you, God of all, Father of all, honour and glory, thanks and praise, worship and adoration, now and in every age, for ever and ever.

Congregation: Amen. You are the fullness of reality, one without a second, being, knowledge, bliss! OM, TAT, SAT![3]

The bread and wine or the chapatti and water are lifted and offered with the words of the consecration from the Roman Missal.

Silence follows.

The sign of peace is offered to all present and the bread and wine passed around for those who want to take communion.

Silence follows.

Final prayer and blessing:

> *May this Eucharist bring joy and peace to all*
> *humanity and to all sentient beings.*
> *May the Lord who provides full understanding*
> *empty our minds to a new humanity.*
> *May the unity of the Trinity bring forth in all of us the*
> *unity of humanity and the whole of creation.*

*May we be the bridge and the raft for all those
who suffer. Amen. OM TAT TA.*

Silence and meditation follow.

CHRISTIAN–HINDU LITURGIES (MIDDAY WORSHIP)

Those attending sit on the floor and the midday prayer starts with silence.

A Psalm is read.

A reading from another tradition follows – for example:

> Even as a spider sends forth and draws in its threat, even as plants arise from the earth and hairs from the body of man, even so the whole creation arises from the Eternal.[1]

> For sentient beings, poor and destitute, may I become a treasure ever-plentiful, and lie before them closely in their reach, a varied source of all that they might need.[2]

> For when he dies, and they place him on the fire, then he is born out of the fire, and then the fire consumes only his body. And just as he is born from his father or from his mother, in that very way he is born from the fire.[3]

Silence follows.

The midday prayer ends with the following prayer:

Celebrant: In the Oneness of the Supreme Spirit through Christ who unites all things in his fullness we and the whole creation give to you, God of all, Father of all, honour and glory, thanks and praise, worship and adoration, now and in every age, for ever and ever.

Congregation: Amen. You are the fullness of reality, one without a second, being, knowledge, bliss! OM, TAT, SAT![4]

Appendix 6

DECLARATIONS ON A SHARED HUMANITY: ST ANDREWS AND INDIA

Recently, the efforts for a common journey in the commonality of silence arising from Arunachala Hermitage (Anstruther) were realized in the fostering of two 'Declarations' that outlined a common journey for different faiths with the understanding that first and foremost we are human beings. As 'Declarations', these documents were not legal agreements, treatises or canons but common agreements for an ongoing journey.

THE ST ANDREWS DECLARATION

The first 'Declaration' on a shared humanity was signed on 23 September 2016 at the University of St Andrews in the context of a conference on silence in Christianity, Buddhism and Hinduism. Thus, religious leaders, diplomats, academics, members of faith communities, school representatives, members of NGOs and interfaith practitioners gathered at the University of St Andrews in Scotland to publicly assert the basic common denominator of all members of faith communities, of all those who are atheists or agnostics, including Buddhists and Hindus, indeed the whole of humanity. Any encounter, be it religious or purely humanistic, requires the will to do so. In that will there is the firm purpose of accepting similarities and differences, diverse actions and diverse traditions, knowing that by accepting that God is the Absolute and that the Absolute has millions of manifestations we can encounter some of those human manifestations along the road.

It was at Arunachala Hermitage in the context of prayer that I wrote in November 2015 the basics of what such a will of journeying together could be. I knew that the central encounter on a journey happens within a mystical language, the language of God that many times cannot be embodied by the human language, the everyday language of our human encounter. Within such predication of human language, I chose some basic texts that are central to the main religions of this world, texts that divide us, but texts that are recited, believed and treasured within our common journey, a journey that unites us. The 'Declaration' sets the parameter of human beings as equals in a journey, not in isolation but with others, and the final text was first published in electronic form as part of the interfaith year that coincided with the 2015–2016 academic year at the University of St Andrews.[1]

This 'Declaration', published in a shorter form in June 2016, was expanded with just one more paragraph that included a Sikh text after my visit to Guru Nanak Dev University in Amritsar, Punjab, India, during that same month. Thus, the second version of the 'St Andrews Declaration' with the addition of paragraph 7 reads as follows:

1. We declare that human beings are born equal and that they all share hopes and aspirations, paths of fulfilment, paths of suffering, and dreams within a common journey as human beings.

2. We declare that human beings share the freedom to follow particular paths of life within the rights and obligations shared by all and contributing to the common good of humanity.

3. We declare our respect and good-will towards all religious traditions that follow a path towards peace, common cooperation, and goodness.

4. We share a common path towards the Absolute and as such we recognize the diversity of paths, texts and traditions that we intend to respect and foster their respect in others.

5. 'For sentient beings, poor and destitute, may I become a treasure ever plentiful, and lie before them closely in their reach, a varied source of all that they might need' (Shantideva, The Way of the Bodhisattva III, 10).

6. 'OM. This eternal Word is all: what was, what is and what shall be, and what beyond is in eternity. All is OM' (Mandukya Upanishad).

7. 'Blessed is the season when I remember You. Blessed is that work which is done for You. Blessed is that heart in which You dwell, O Giver of all. O my God! You are the Universal Father of us all. You dwell deep within each and every heart. All share in Your Grace; none are beyond You' (Sri Guru Granth Sahib, p.97).

8. 'Shema Yisrael, Adonai eloheinu, Adonai echad – barukh shem kevod malkhuto le'olam va'ed' (Deuteronomy 6.4–9).

9. 'In the name of God, the Gracious, the Merciful, Praise be to God, Lord of the Worlds, the Most Gracious, the Most Merciful' (al-Fatihah).

10. 'May they all be one, just as, Father, you are in me and I am in you, so that they also may be in us, so that the world may believe it was you who sent me' (John 17.21).

11. We declare that as brothers and sisters we can share our joy, peace and happiness with all human beings through our daily prayer and meditation.[2]

The Declaration was launched on the morning of Friday 23 September 2016 at the University of St Andrews, coinciding with the conference 'Silence, Texts and Service: Towards a Christian, Hindu and Buddhist Dialogue'. The event was attended by senior members of the Christian churches, the Catholic Church, Hindu communities from the UK and India, senior Buddhist monks and an Edinburgh imam. The 130-strong religious delegation from 19 countries was joined by 32 school pupils from Fife, Scotland, and three school children from Canada. The Declaration, publically signed, suggested to those watching the ceremony that religious tenets provide the solution to radicalization and violence within contemporary society, if those tenets are taken seriously.

I addressed the following words to those participating in the signing ceremony and those who followed the ceremony via the internet:

Venerable Abbot Rimpoche, Imam Yahya, Moderator of the General Assembly of the Church of Scotland, representatives of Pope Francis and of H.H. the 14th Dalai Lama, members of the delegations from Austria, Canada, Norway and India, Master of the United College, Principal of St Mary's College, Fr Clooney SJ, distinguished excellencies, fellow pilgrims and fellow human beings. I would like to greet those who are following our gathering through the internet, particularly those at the Vatican (Papa Francisco, un gran abrazo), in Norway, and at the hills of Dharamsala, Tashi Delek! I welcome you to the University of St Andrews, the first university of Scotland, a place that has fostered dialogue and academic colloquia for the past 600 years. It has been my dream and desire that we should meet in St Andrews to continue conversations that began over the past few years, particularly in India. Those of you coming from Amritsar would know my joy of having spent time with you last June and having visited the Golden Temple and two institutions of dialogue and learning. I am very thankful and moved by the response of more than one hundred guests who have arrived to share reflections, to learn from each other, to start a way of ongoing cooperation, to pray together for peace and understanding and to dispense greetings beside the St Andrews Pier to many fellow human beings that will gather in India next year. In gathering together, we suggest publicly to civil society that members of faith communities have a lot to offer to contemporary society, that the practice of an honest path of symbolic belonging brings cooperation, peace and understanding to our own societies, nations and the contemporary world. The path of violence and hate is not our path and it cannot be the path that arises out of reading sacred texts, prayer and meditation. Your choice of being present has not been easy. That I know. With many of you I have shared pilgrimages, conversations, meals and mutual understanding. The signing of the St Andrews Declaration for a Shared Humanity is the affirmation that we agree on disagreeing but that in our diversity and our different paths we can agree that at the basic level we are all human beings. Through the 11 paragraphs of the Declaration we call upon our fellow human beings to adhere to this basic tenet and to respect all human beings and all sentient beings. During the conversations that will follow the signing of the St Andrews Declaration we will examine the contribution of silence within Christianity, Buddhism and Hinduism. These three traditions proclaim the centrality of the action for other human beings, all sentient beings, and our planet as well as the cosmos. This common journey departs from a single way of material life and through the principles of metaphysical causation and the inclusion of all human beings shares the joy and the suffering of all sentient beings through respect, compassion and a common understanding. If we sign a document it is to express a common understanding, our walking together visiting each other and praying together continues as it already started. This is a journey that continues because it has already started in the places where we live our daily lives and will continue through periodic encounters in each other's symbolic spaces. In a year's time, we will be gathering in India to sign the India Declaration in the land of Hinduism and where the Tibetan Buddhist community and the Christian Churches have also found a home. A common silence during our journey will become our common language. For it is through silence and the calming of my unwanted emotions that I wait for another human being and this visitor becomes a divine presence and a visiting manifestation of the divine. Silence provides the creative movement of opening to others in which otherness becomes closeness and closeness becomes happiness. Through the St Andrews Declaration, we reject the misuse of our dear symbolic systems for violence, hate and exclusion. Killing, hate and violence contradict completely the tenets of our religious beliefs and of our way of life and we condemn such violence. It is never acceptable to harm another human being, it is never acceptable to harm a sentient being, it is never acceptable to harm mother earth or Mama Ganga. We seek refuge in the possibility of meditating together and through the active engagement with public society to do good, and to generate positive energies, dialogue and understanding. We serve the poor and the marginalized through our places of worship and we embrace others because of their beauty and sanctity.

This morning our solidarity goes to those who wanted to be present but couldn't come and those who feared that by being associated with the signing of the Declaration they and their families would be harmed. Among us there are wise and holy religious leaders, great teachers and students of this university, researchers and fellow human beings. But we have invited those who represent the hope of peace for the nations. Thus, I welcome the representatives of the secondary schools in the kingdom of Fife. Take this opportunity to share our commitment to peace and understanding with others, show your happiness through your selfies and social networks, because it is you who now can make the difference towards a more inclusive and ethical world. I also welcome our Canadian pilgrims from Quebec. You have insisted that Canadians wanted to take part, and I am delighted that we can welcome the youngest signatories of the Declaration: Charles and Pierre, bienvenu! This is an academic endeavour in which we will fight ignorance through knowledge and we will come to learn other ways, other texts and other silences because it is through knowledge and the discussion of ideas that our humanity can feel a basic togetherness.

THE INDIA DECLARATION

It was in Amritsar, India, after visiting the Golden Temple, a sacred place for the Sikhs, that I wrote in dialogue with my life companion the India Declaration on a Shared Humanity during June 2016. In Amritsar, where a massacre of Indian civilians under the British Raj had taken place, and where the violence of the partition of India divided Hindus and Muslims, I prayed hard for peace and unity among human beings on the same journey. The final text was reached with two corrections in form after a conversation with Ramesh Babu and family and with the wise and patient advice of Kabir Babu.

The signing of the 'India Declaration', in June 2017, in Delhi, Amritsar and Dharamsala, will follow the same pattern of thought, prayer and contemplation of the St Andrews Declaration: a common humanity in a common journey of a shared symbolic significance with material and textual differences but made in common. The text as corrected in conversation with Kabir Babu reads as follows:

1. We locate ourselves today in India

   Mother and path of all religions

   And secular experiences.

2. We locate ourselves in the land

   Of many religions and many philosophies

   And together we proclaim

   A shared common humanity.

3. We embrace those who suffer

   Particularly those who suffer

   Any kind of unjust violence

   And discrimination in the name of religion.

4. We greet the Absolute as our guide

   As our principle and together we seek

   Human and spiritual immortality.

5. We stand with India, the land of Gandhiji

   And the land of Mother Theresa of Kolkata

   And we seek to embrace the poor,

   The marginalized and the oppressed.

6. May the OM TAT TA resound

   In our hearts and in the hearts of

   All Indians as bearers of a shared humanity.

7. May our lives, prayers and meditations

    From Kashmir to Kanyakumari

    Give praise to the Absolute and Eternal.

8. We stand together for a future understanding of peoples

    And we pledge our thoughts and actions

    To foster peace and religious understanding.

9. May India remain a sign of all history

    And all future history of peace and human understanding.

    OM TAT TA. Amen.[3]

NOTES

ACKNOWLEGEMENTS

1 Mario I. Aguilar (1998) *Being Oromo in Kenya*. Trenton, NJ: Africa World Press.

2 Carlo Carretto (2007) *Essential Writings*, selected and edited by Robert Ellsberg. Maryknoll, NY: Orbis.

INTRODUCTION

1 Mario I. Aguilar (2016) 'Introduction: Dialogues in History, Dialogues in Hinduism', in Mario I. Aguilar, *Christian Ashrams, Hindu Caves and Sacred Rivers: Christian–Hindu Monastic Dialogue in India 1950–1993*. London and Philadelphia: Jessica Kingsley Publishers, pp.11–26.

2 Aguilar, 'Introduction: Dialogues in History, Dialogues in Hinduism', p.11.

3 For an assessment of that constancy of the cenobium, and the political and the private life of Thomas Merton, see Mario I. Aguilar (2011) 'Hermit and Activist', in Mario I. Aguilar, *Thomas Merton: Contemplation and Political Action*. London: SPCK, pp.61–75.

4 Joseph Wong (2002) 'The Threefold Good: Romualdian Charism and Monastic Tradition', in Peter-Damian Belisle (ed.) *The Privilege of Love: Camaldolese Benedictine Spirituality*. Collegeville, MN: Liturgical Press, pp.81–97 at p.88.

5 Benedicta Ward (1975) *Sayings of the Desert Fathers*. Kalamazoo, MI: Cistercian Publications, p.139.

6 Robert Hale (2002) 'Koinonia: The Privilege of Love', in Belisle (ed.) *The Privilege of Love*, pp.99–114 at p.105.

7 Mario I. Aguilar, Notes and Records, 11 June 2016. (My unpublished research notes.)

8 Sri Harimandir Sahib (n.d.) Available at www.goldentempleamritsar.org, accessed on 28 November 2016.

9 Sri Harimandir Sahib (n.d.).

10 Gurnam Singh Sanghera (2013) 'Religious harmony – a Sikh perspective', *Perspectives on Guru Granth Sahib 8*, 67–84 at 73.

11 Guru Granth Sahib, p.1299.

12 Aguilar, Notes and Records, 11 June 2016.

13 Aguilar, Notes and Records, 12 June 2016.

14 Aguilar, *Christian Ashrams, Hindu Caves and Sacred Rivers*.

15 See Panikkar's full argument interpreted in Aguilar (2016) 'Silence, the Pro-Logos and the Monk in Raimon Panikkar', in *Christian Ashrams, Hindu Caves and Sacred Rivers*, pp.143–58.

16 Raimon Panikkar (2014) 'The Archetype of the Monk', in *Mysticism and Spirituality: Spirituality – the Way of Life, Opera Omnia I.2*. Maryknoll, NY: Orbis, pp.133–44 at p.137.

17 I have outlined some theoretical principles for a Christian–Buddhist dialogue in Mario I. Aguilar (2012) *Church, Liberation and World Religions: Towards a Christian–Buddhist Dialogue, Ecclesiological Investigations 14*. London: Bloomsbury.

18 I return to the work of Gurnam Singh Sanghera, where we are reminded by a Sikh of how our Christian tenets, if considered exclusive of others, provide a tremendous globalized problem. He writes: 'Exclusivistic attitude is the view that Christianity is the only authentic religion and that other religions are spurious', and reminds us that Pope John Paul II undermined the tenets of Vatican II regarding the non-rejection of any religion by the Catholic Church (see Gurnam Singh Sanghera (2013) 'Religious harmony – a Sikh perspective', pp.80–1). For an outline of Vatican II's statements on other religions see Aguilar, 'Dialogue in Vatican II', in *Church, Liberation and World Religions*, pp.16–35, and 'Christianity and Hinduism', pp.27–31. I note that exclusivist approaches have been challenged by inclusivist approaches to the world religions. Douglas Pratt's contribution to these debates vis-à-vis pluralism has argued that 'the relationship between the universal and a multiplicity of religions is problematic'; see Douglas Pratt (2007) 'Pluralism, postmodernism and interreligious dialogue', *Sophia 46*, 243–59 at 258.

19 Visit to the Cascade Centre for Education in Aguilar, Notes and Records, 13 June 2016.

20 I focus here on the dialogue, aesthetic, poetic and philosophical, that took place on 13 June 2014 in Amritsar, while further larger conversations with Kabir Babu are explored in Chapter 3, including his poetry.

21 Visit to the Babu family (Amritsar) in Aguilar, Notes and Records, 12 June 2016.

22 *The Hundred Thousand Songs of Milarepa* (1999), translated and annotated by Garma C.C. Chang. Boston and London: Shambhala.

23 Raimon Panikkar (2010) *The Rhythm of Being: The Unbroken Trinity, The Gifford Lectures, Edinburgh University*. Maryknoll, NY: Orbis, p.249.

24 Anthony de Mello SJ (1983) *The Song of the Bird*. Anand, Gujarat: Gujarat Sahitya Prakash.

25 De Mello, *The Song of the Bird*, p.xv.

26 De Mello, *The Song of the Bird*, pp.4–5 at p.5.

27 For Pope Francis' encounters with the poor and the marginalized, and his interfaith dialogue, particularly with Jews and Muslims in Buenos Aires, see Mario I. Aguilar (2014) *Pope Francis: His Life and Thought*. Cambridge: Lutterworth, especially 'Inter-Faith and Inter-Religious Dialogue' at pp.171–7. For his conversations with a rabbi see Jorge Bergoglio and Abraham Skorka (2013) *Sobre el cielo y la tierra*. New York: Vintage Español (original edition published by Random House Mondadori, Buenos Aires, 2010).

28 Junno Arocho Esteves (2016) 'Pope Francis washes feet of refugees on Holy Thursday', *Catholic Herald*, 24 March. Available at www.catholicherald.co.uk/news/2016/03/24/pope-francis-washes-feet-of-refugees-on-holy-thursday, accessed on 28 November 2016.

29 'Final Declaration of the Colloquium in Rome of the Pontifical Council for Interreligious Dialogue and the Royal Institute for Inter-Faith Studies (R.I.I.F.S.)', Holy See Press Office N.0322, 7 May 2016.

30 Catechism of the Catholic Church (1994) London: Geoffrey Chapman, §920 and Codex Iuris Canonici (1983), canon 603, §1.

31 Donald Nicholl (1991) 'Other Religions (Nostra Aetate)', in Adrian Hastings (ed.) *Modern Catholicism: Vatican II and After*. London: SPCK, and New York: Oxford University Press, pp.126–34 at p.126.

32 See, for example, Elie Wiesel (2008) *The Night Trilogy: Night/Dawn/Day*. New York: Hill and Wang.

33 Rosemary Radford Ruether (1999) 'The Holocaust: Theological and Ethical Reflections', in Gregory Baum (ed.) *The Twentieth Century: A Theological Overview*. Maryknoll, NY: Orbis, Ottawa: Novalis, and London: Geoffrey Chapman, pp.76–90 at p.88.

34 Ruether, 'The Holocaust', p.88.

35 Bal K. Gupta (2012) *Forgotten Atrocities: Memoirs of a Survivor of the 1947 Partition of India*. Raleigh, NC: Lulu Enterprises.

CHAPTER 1

1   Bede Griffiths (1965, 1984) *Christ in India: Essays towards a Hindu–Christian Dialogue*. Springfield, IL: Templegate Publishers, pp.46–7, reproduced in (2004) *Bede Griffiths: Essential Writings*, selected with an introduction by Thomas Matus. Maryknoll, NY: Orbis, p.65.

2   Mario I. Aguilar, Nalanda Hermitage Diary (NHD), 13 July 2016. (My unpublished personal diary.)

3   For other Christian monks within the Indian tradition see Mario I. Aguilar (2016) *Christian Ashrams, Hindu Caves and Sacred Rivers: Christian–Hindu Monastic Dialogue in India 1950–1993*. London and Philadelphia: Jessica Kingsley Publishers.

4   Raimon Panikkar (2010) *The Rhythm of Being: The Unbroken Trinity, The Gifford Lectures, Edinburgh University*. Maryknoll, NY: Orbis, p.337.

5   For further biographical references on the life of Charles de Foucauld, see Charles Hillyer (1990) *Charles de Foucauld*. Collegeville, MN: Liturgical Press; Charles Lepetit (1983) *Two Dancers in the Desert: The Life of Charles de Foucauld*. Tunbridge Wells: Burns & Oates, and Maryknoll, NY: Orbis; Marion Mill Preminger (1961) *The Sands of Tamanrasset*. New York: Hawthorn Books; Jean-François Six (1965) *Witness in the Desert: The Life of Charles de Foucauld*. New York: Macmillan; and Margaret Trouncer (1972) *Charles de Foucauld*. London: George G. Harrap.

6   For the history of the Tuareg in Algeria, see Douglas Porch (1986) *The Conquest of the Sahara*. New York: Fromm International Publishing.

7   André Basset (ed.) *Poésies Tourègues: Dialecte de l'Ahaggar*, recueillies par le P. de Foucauld. Paris: E. Leroux, vol. I, 1925, vol. II, 1930.

8   Robert Ellsberg (1999) 'Introduction: Little Brother of Jesus', in *Charles de Foucauld: Essential Writings*. Maryknoll, NY: Orbis, pp.13–29 at p.22.

9   Before Vatican II (1962–1965) the Mass was said in Latin with the celebrant facing the altar rather than the congregation. Due to the very detailed instructions on how to celebrate the Mass, the celebrant needed the help of a trained server. Without such a server and without a consecrated altar that could be constituted by a consecrated stone or a saint's relic, Mass could not be lawfully celebrated. Abhishiktananda faced the same dilemma in India as he carried an altar stone always in order to celebrate the Mass, to the amusement of his friend Raimon Panikkar; see Raimon Panikkar (2014) 'Letter to Abhisiktananda on Eastern and Western Monasticism', in *Mysticism and Spirituality: Spirituality – The Way of Life, Opera Omnia, I.2*. Maryknoll, NY: Orbis, pp.253–77.

10 Ellsberg, 'Introduction: Little Brother of Jesus', p.13.

11 The Sanusiya were a mystical order within Islam founded by the Grand Sanusi, an outstanding intellectual of North Africa, in the nineteenth century; see B.G. Martin (1976) *Muslim Brotherhoods in Nineteenth Century Africa*. Cambridge: Cambridge University Press.

12 Paris: Editions Chalet, 1975. English translation by Zoe Hersov published as *Christian Hermit in an Islamic World: A Muslim's View of Charles de Foucauld*. New York and Mahwah, NJ: Paulist Press, 1999.

13 Merad, 'Preface', *Christian Hermit in an Islamic World*, pp.13–18 at p.14.

14 Merad, 'Preface', p.14.

15 Merad, 'Preface', p.15.

16 Merad, 'The Encounter with Islam', in *Christian Hermit in an Islamic World*, pp.44–57 at p.44. Merad refers to Louis Massignon (1883–1962), a pioneer in Christian–Muslim relations, who in 1919 was appointed to the Chair of Muslim Sociology and Sociography at the Collège de France, a chair he finally occupied in 1926. Massignon was invited by Charles de Foucauld to join him at Tamanrasset, an offer he declined. Instead he got married and later became a Franciscan Tertiary with the name of Ibrahim. In 1949 and with the permission of Pope Pius XII, Massignon became a Melkite Greek Catholic, one of a community of Arab Catholics who celebrate the liturgy under the Byzantine rite. Massignon was the executor of Charles' spiritual legacy and he saw the difficult process to negotiate its imprimatur by the Vatican. The result of this was the Directoire, published in 1928 – the Rule for the Foundation of the Little Brothers of Jesus.

17 Merad, 'Conclusion: The Strait Way', in *Christian Hermit in an Islamic World*, pp.70–5 at p.73. Merad is citing from René Bazin (1921) *Charles de Foucauld – Explorateur du Maroc – Ermite au Sahara*. Paris: Plon, p.466.

18 The *amenukal* is the supreme elected chief of a Tuareg confederation.

19 Merad, 'Happiness in the Imitation of Jesus', in *Christian Hermit in an Islamic World*, pp.19–25 at p.25. Merad is citing from Bazin, *Charles de Foucauld*, p.393.

20 'Translator's Foreword', in *Christian Hermit in an Islamic World*, pp.1–9 at p.7. Zoe Hersov is citing from Bazin, *Charles de Foucauld*, p.446.

21 Six, *Witness in the Desert*, pp.51–3.

22 Ellsberg, 'Preface', *Charles de Foucauld: Essential Writings*, pp.9–11 at p.10.

23 Carlo Carretto (1990) *Letters from the Desert*, 30th anniversary edn. London: Darton, Longman & Todd, and (1979) *The Desert in the City*. London and Glasgow: William Collins.

24 For a selection of Carretto's writings see Robert Ellsberg (ed.) (2007) *Carlo Carretto: Essential Writings*. Maryknoll, NY: Orbis Books.

25 When I met my life companion at a parish in Santiago, we spent many happy and meaningful hours discussing our reading of Carretto's *Letters from the Desert* at her terraza. It was clear for us that we could grow in our dreams through the desert and that there was a possible way of recreating the desert in our own places and in the midst of political turmoil, violations of human rights and the negation of the Church's place in the life of society.

26 Raimon Panikkar, 'The Monk according to Hindū Scriptures', in *Opera Omnia I.2*, p.234. Original text published as 'Le moine selon les écritures de l'hindouisme', in *Les Moines chrétiens face aux religions d'Asie*. Bangalore: AMC, 1973, pp.80–91.

27 Panikkar, 'The Monk according to Hindū Scriptures', p.234.

28 Sri Ramana Maharshi (n.d.). Available at www.sriramanamaharshi.org, accessed on 28 November 2016.

29 'Preface', in Arthur Osborne (ed.) (1997) *The Collected Works of Ramana Maharshi*. York Beach, ME: Red Wheel/Weiser, pp.7–13 at p.7.

30 Shirley Du Boulay (2005) *The Cave of the Heart: The Life of Swami Abhishiktananda*. Maryknoll, NY: Orbis, p.67.

31 Paul Brunton (2012) *A Search in Secret India*. Eastford, CT: Martino Fine Books; Somerset Maugham (2003) *The Razor's Edge*. London: Vintage.

32 'Preface' in Osborne, *Collected Works of Ramana Maharshi*, p.11.

33 In later writings Maharshi eliminated breathing exercises or yoga as paths to liberating the self; see for example 'Devikalottara' §16: 'If you desire eternal *Moksha*, do not engage in Yogic practices or incantations, or anything else of the kind', and §17: 'there is no worship, or prayer, or incantation, or meditation. There is nothing to be known apart from the Self.' The full text of the 'Devikalottara' is available in Osborne, *Collected Works of Ramana Maharshi*, pp.111–17.

34 Maharshi, *Self-Enquiry*, 'The Nature of the Mind', in Osborne, *Collected Works of Ramana Maharshi*, pp.20–2 at p.21.

35 Maharshi, *Self-Enquiry*, 'Enquiry into the Self', in Osborne, *Collected Works of Ramana Maharshi*, pp.18–20 at p.19.

36 Maharshi, *Self-Enquiry*, 'The Supreme Being Is the Self', in Osborne, *Collected Works of Ramana Maharshi*, pp.26–7 at p.27.

37 Maharshi, *Self-Enquiry*, 'Worship Is Only Self-Enquiry', in Osborne, *Collected Works of Ramana Maharshi*, pp.28–9 at p.29.

38 Maharshi, *Self-Enquiry*, 'Liberation', in Osborne, *Collected Works of Ramana Maharshi*, pp.30–3 at p.32.

39 Maharshi, *Self-Enquiry*, 'The Eightfold Path of Yoga', in Osborne, *Collected Works of Ramana Maharshi*, pp.33–6 at p.35.

40 Maharshi, *Self-Enquiry*, 'The Eightfold Path of Yoga', p.35.

41 Maharshi, *Self-Enquiry*, 'The Eightfold Path of Yoga', p.36.

42 Maharshi, *Self-Enquiry*, 'Renunciation', in Osborne, *Collected Works of Ramana Maharshi*, p.38.

43 For some of Maharshi's teachings see John David (formerly Premananda) (2007) *Arunachala Talks: Spiritual Wisdom Offered in a Direct Simple Expression to Touch Your Heart*. London: Open Sky Press.

44 Maharshi, *Who Am I?*, in Osborne, *Collected Works of Ramana Maharshi*, pp.39–47. Text and commentary also available in John David (formerly

Premananda) (2009) *Arunachala Shiva: Commentaries on Sri Ramana Maharshi's Teachings. 'Who Am I?'* London: Open Sky Press.

45 Maharshi, 'The Marital Garland of Letters', in Osborne, *Collected Works of Ramana Maharshi*, pp.52–60.

46 Maharshi, 'The Marital Garland of Letters', §108.

47 Maharshi, 'Sri Arunachala Mahatmya: The Glory of Sri Arunachala', in Osborne, *Collected Works of Ramana Maharshi*, p.51.

48 Maharshi, 'The Necklet of Nine Gems', §7, in Osborne, *Collected Works of Ramana Maharshi*, pp.61–2.

49 Maharshi, 'Eleven Verses on Sri Arunachala', §9, in Osborne, *Collected Works of Ramana Maharshi*, pp.62–4.

50 Maharshi, 'Sri Arunachala Ashtakam: Eight Stanzas on Sri Arunachala', §6, in Osborne, *Collected Works of Ramana Maharshi*, pp.65–7.

51 For a short biography see Charles E. Moore (2005) 'Introduction', *Sadhu Sundar Singh: Essential Writings.* Maryknoll, NY: Orbis, pp.9–29. Other works include C.F. Andrews (1934) *Sadhu Sundar Singh: A Personal Memoir.* London: Hodder & Stoughton; A.J. Appasamy (1958) *Sundar Singh: A Biography.* London: Lutterworth; Friedrich Heiler (1996) *The Gospel of Sadhu Sundar Singh.* Delhi: ISPCK; and Phyllis Thompson (1992) *Sadhu Sundar Singh.* Bromley: O.M. Publishing.

52 Moore, 'Introduction', *Sadhu Sundar Singh: Essential Writings*, p.18.

53 Moore, 'Introduction', p.26.

54 Selections from these six books are available in Moore, *Sadhu Sundar Singh: Essential Writings*, Part I: 'Conversations', pp.31–101, and Part II: 'Parables', pp.103–41.

55 Abhishiktananda (1967) *Une messe aux sources du Gange.* Paris: Le Seuil, translated (1967) as *The Mountain of the Lord: Pilgrimage to Gangotri.* Bangalore: CISRS; reprinted (1974) in *Guru and Disciple.* London: SPCK; new edition (1990) Delhi: ISPCK; Italian edition (1968) *Una messa alle sorgenti del Ganga.* Brescia: Morcelliana.

56 Abhishiktananda to Mme O. Baumer-Despeigne, 1 October 1968. A selection of Abhishiktananda's letters are published in James Stuart (1989) *Swāmi Abhishiktānanda: His Life Told Through His Letters.* New Delhi: ISPCK.

57 Abhishiktananda to Mrs Anne-Marie Stokes, 24 November 1968.

58 Abhishiktananda to Mme O. Baumer-Despeigne, 24 November 1968.

59 Abhishiktananda to Canon J. Lemarié, 14 November 1968.

60 Abhishiktananda to Mme O. Baumer-Despeigne, 23 January 1969. He refers to his 1965 work *Sagesse hindoue mystique chrétienne: du Védanta à la Trinité.* Paris: Centurion; English translations with additions and revisions (1974, 1984, 1990) *Saccidānanda: A Christian Approach to Advaitic Experience.* Delhi: ISPCK.

61 Abhishiktananda to Mrs Anne-Marie Stokes, 25 January 1969. He expanded on the possible use of Hindu texts in the liturgy in (1973) 'Hindu Scriptures and worship', *Word and Worship VI*, 6–7, 187–95 and 243–53.

62 Abhishiktananda to Canon J. Lemarié, 17 December 1968.

63 *Examiner*, 9 November 1968, with correspondence until the end of the year and editorials on 16 and 30 November 1968. See Abhishiktananda to Canon J. Lemarié, 24 January 1969.

64 Abhishiktananda (1976) *Hindu–Christian Meeting Point – within the Cave of the Heart*. Delhi: ISPCK (originally published in 1969); (1970) *Meeting Point and Towards the Renewal of the Indian Church*. Bangalore: Dharmaram College.

65 *Report. All India Seminar: Church in India Today*, New Delhi, 1969.

66 *New Orders of the Mass for India*. Bangalore: NBCLC, 1974, pp.63ff.

67 S. Grant, 'Swamiji – the Man', *Clergy Monthly 38*, 11, 487–8.

68 Abhishiktananda to Raimon Panikkar, 25 June 1969.

69 Abhishiktananda to Canon J. Lemarié, 10 June 1969.

70 Abhishiktananda to Canon J. Lemarié, 20 July 1969.

71 In the conclusions to his work Panikkar suggested two important markers for the development of a theology of the world religions: 'God is at work in all religions: the Christian kerygma does not proclaim a new God, but the mirabilia of God, of which the mystery of Christ hidden in God is the *alpha* and *omega*', and 'Whatever God does *ad extra* happens through Christ'; see Raimundo [Raimon] Panikkar (1981) *The Unknown Christ of Hinduism: Towards an Ecumenical Christophany*, rev. and enlarged edn. Maryknoll, NY: Orbis, pp.168–9.

72 Abhishiktananda to Raimon Panikkar, 10 July 1969.

73 Mandukya Upanishad.

74 A personal narrative of Merton's journey through his diaries was published in 1975 as *The Asian Journal of Thomas Merton*, edited by Naomi Burton, Brother Patrick Hart and James Laughlin. New York: New Directions.

75 Brother Patrick Hart (1975) 'Foreword', in *The Asian Journal of Thomas Merton*, pp.xxi–xxix at p.xxii.

76 Merton had written some studies on St Bernard, collected in *Thomas Merton on St. Bernard*, Cistercian Studies Series 9. Kalamazoo, MI: Cistercian Publications, and London and Oxford: A.R. Mowbray, 1980.

77 Entry for 15 December 1967 in Patrick Hart OCSO (ed.) (1999) *The Other Side of the Mountain: The Journals of Thomas Merton, Vol. 7 1967–1968*. New York: HarperCollins, p.20.

78 Michael Mott (1984) *The Seven Mountains of Thomas Merton*. Boston, MA: Houghton-Mifflin, p.25.

79 For a fruitful exploration of this period see Bob Baker and Gray Henry (eds) (1999) *Merton and Sufism, the Untold Story: A Complete Compendium.* Louisville, KY: Fons Vitae, and Bonnie Thurston (2004) 'Some Reflections on Islamic Poems by Thomas Merton', in Angus Stuart (ed.) *Thomas Merton: The World in my Bloodstream.* Papers from the 2002 Oakham Conference of the Thomas Merton Society of Great Britain & Ireland. Abergavenny: Three Peaks Press, pp.40–53.

80 'Aziz, Abdul', in William H. Shannon, Christine M. Bochen and Patrick F. O'Connell (eds) (2002) *The Thomas Merton Encyclopedia.* Maryknoll, NY: Orbis, p.20.

81 Mott, *The Seven Mountains of Thomas Merton*, p.432.

82 Mott, *The Seven Mountains of Thomas Merton*, p.432.

83 During 1966 Joan Baez visited Merton and tried to convince him to leave Gethsemani and to join a larger world of peace activism; see Lawrence S. Cunningham (1999) *Thomas Merton & the Monastic Vision.* Grand Rapids, MI, and Cambridge: William B. Eerdmans, p.139.

84 Entry for 21 January 1968 in Hart, *The Other Side of the Mountain*, p.44.

85 Entry for 4 January 1968 in Hart, *The Other Side of the Mountain*, p.33.

86 Entry for 5 January 1968 in Hart, *The Other Side of the Mountain*, p.33.

87 Mott, *The Seven Mountains of Thomas Merton*, p.433.

88 Mott, *The Seven Mountains of Thomas Merton*, p.433.

89 For a good biographical historiography of Merton's spiritual development see Cunningham, *Thomas Merton & the Monastic Vision.*

90 The essay appeared in Thomas Merton (1960) *Disputed Questions.* New York: Farrar, Straus and Cudahy, pp.177–207, published a year after Pope John XXIII's call for a new Vatican Council. For a commentary on the essay see William R. Shannon (1994) 'Reflections on Thomas Merton's article: Notes for Philosophy of Solitude', *Cistercian Studies Quarterly 29*, 1.

91 Thomas Merton (1965) *The Way of Chuang Tzu.* New York: New Directions; (1967) *Mystics and Zen Masters.* New York: Farrar, Straus and Company; (1968) *Zen and the Birds of Appetite.* New York: New Directions.

92 The three meetings between Merton and the Dalai Lama are described in Merton's diary; see entries of 4–8 November 1968 in Hart, *The Other Side of the Mountain*, pp.250–66.

CHAPTER 2

1 On 14 December 1967 Merton writes in his diary: 'Yesterday – after confession a short conversation with Fr. Matthew [Kelty] about the coming abbatial election. Later, after dinner, Brother Job [Maurer] walked

up with me to the hermitage to talk about his departure (soon), and while we drank some of his oversweet blackberry wine this conversation turned to the abbatial election too' (in Patrick Hart (ed.) (1999) *The Other Side of the Mountain: The Journals of Thomas Merton, Vol. 7 1967–1968*. New York: HarperCollins, p.24).

2   It is remarkable that at the time of Thomas Merton there were three or four hermits at any given time. Merton lived in a small bungalow, while there was somebody else in a trailer. On 28 November 1967 Merton wrote: 'Yesterday afternoon I walked over to see Fr. Hilarion in his trailer. It was quiet and sunny. He is very happy and relaxed there, very much changed (as far as his mood goes – no more strain and tension) and seems completely satisfied' (Hart, *The Other Side of the Mountain*, p.18).

3   James Stuart (1989) *Swāmi Abhishiktānanda: His Life Told Through His Letters*. New Delhi: ISPCK, p.69.

4   Cited in Stuart, *Swāmi Abhishiktānanda*, p.67.

5   Carlo Carretto (1972) *Letters from the Desert*. Maryknoll, NY: Orbis, and London: Darton, Longman & Todd, p.92. For the development of such a spiritual desert as experienced by Carretto in the Algerian desert and later implanted within the urban centres of Europe, see *Carlo Carretto: Essential Writings*, selected with an introduction by Robert Ellsberg. Maryknoll, NY: Orbis, 2007.

6   For a full introduction to *Vedānta* see Christopher Bartley (2015) *An Introduction to Indian Philosophy: Hindu and Buddhist Ideas from Original Sources*. London: Bloomsbury, ch. 10, pp.175–80.

7   Bartley, *An Introduction to Indian Philosophy*, p.175.

8   For the history, interpretation and samples of Upanishadic texts see 'Renunciation in the Upanishads 600–200 BCE', in Wendy Doniger (2015) *Hinduism: The Norton Anthology of World Religions*, ed. Jack Miles. New York: W.W. Norton, pp.105–6.

9   Doniger, *Hinduism*, p.105.

10   Doniger, *Hinduism*, p.105.

11   Doniger, *Hinduism*, p.107.

12   For a full introduction to *Advāita Vedānta* see Bartley, *An Introduction to Indian Philosophy*, ch. 11, pp.181–221.

13   Bartley, *An Introduction to Indian Philosophy*, p.182.

14   Abhishiktananda to Canon J. Lemarié, 10 February 1952.

15   Cited in Stuart, *Swāmi Abhishiktānanda*, p.64.

16   Cited in Stuart, *Swāmi Abhishiktānanda*, p.67.

17   Stuart, *Swāmi Abhishiktānanda*, p.68.

18   Abhishiktananda to Canon J. Lemarié, 23 January 1954.

19   In Chapter 5 of this work I attempt a *lectio divina* reading of the Upanishads and *The Way of the Bodhisattva* not in order to solve the

intertextual problems posed by their different epistemologies and ontologies but to show how a Christian can, in the context of a hermitage and of interfaith dialogue, find more manifestations of the Absolute within these daily readings.

20 See Mario I. Aguilar (2012) 'Basic Tenets', in *Church, Liberation and World Religions: Towards a Christian–Buddhist Dialogue, Ecclesiological Investigations 14*. London: Bloomsbury, pp.126–42.

21 Aguilar, *Church, Liberation and World Religions*, p.136.

22 Current work on these marginalized and despised human beings in India includes Eve Rebecca Parker (2016) 'Religious Hybridity in the Brothels of Mathamma: The Sacred Sex Worker and the Dalit Christ', in Peniel Jesudason Rufus Rajkumar and Joseph Prabhakar Dayam (eds) *Many Yet One? Multiple Religious Belonging*. Geneva: World Council of Churches Publications, pp.121–34.

23 The 14th Dalai Lama, 'The Nobel Peace Prize Lecture, Oslo, Norway', in Sidney Piburn (ed.) (1990) *The Dalai Lama: A Policy of Kindness – An Anthology of Writings by and about the Dalai Lama*. Ithaca, NY: Snow Lion Publications, pp.15–25 at p.15.

24 Jon Sobrino (2008) 'Extra Pauperes Nulla Salus: A Short Utopian-Prophetic Essay', in *No Salvation Outside the Poor: Prophetic-Utopian Essays*. Maryknoll, NY: Orbis, pp.35–76 at p.69.

25 Sobrino, *No Salvation Outside the Poor*, p.70.

26 Jizō is the protector of the vulnerable, especially children, travellers and expectant mothers. He is also regarded as the patron deity of deceased children and aborted foetuses, and the saviour of hell-beings. I acknowledge my gratitude to James Morris for this present.

27 Shantideva (2006) *The Way of the Bodhisattva*. Boston and London: Shambhala.

CHAPTER 3

1 See, for example, the 1968 encounters between Thomas Merton and the 14th Dalai Lama in Dharamsala, northern India. In a summary of those three meetings, I outlined three important aspects of such an important moment in Christian–Buddhist dialogue: the commonality of the spiritual experience, the difference of context and path, and the common call to kindness and love for the stranger; see Mario I. Aguilar (2012) 'Thomas Merton and the Dalai Lama', in *Church, Liberation and World Religions: Towards a Christian–Buddhist Dialogue, Ecclesiological Investigations 14*. London: Bloomsbury, pp.87–105.

2 The masterpiece of such silence and dialogue in silence and prayer remains Daniel Berrigan's conversation with Thich Nhat Hanh. Berrigan, a Jesuit,

a poet and a peace activist, met over long midnight conversations with Hanh, a Vietnamese monk and Zen master; see Thich Nhat Hanh and Daniel Berrigan (2001) *The Raft Is Not the Shore: Conversations Towards a Buddhist–Christian Awareness.* Maryknoll, NY: Orbis.

3   On a Catholic understanding of this commonality of joy and suffering see *Gaudium et spes* §1: 'Pastoral Constitution on the Church in the Modern World/ *Gaudium et Spes*', in *Vatican Council II. The Conciliar and Post Conciliar Documents*, ed. Austin Flannery OP, new revised edition. Northport, NY: Costello, and Grand Rapids, MI: William B. Eerdmans, 1992, pp.903–1001. On a Buddhist awareness of other sentient beings see 'The Intermediate Sadhana of the Solitary Hero Vajrabhairava', where, within a self-initiation on 'Four Immeasurables', the practitioner embraces all others in the following words: 'May all sentient beings be endowed with bliss. May all sentient beings be parted from suffering'; see *Self-Initiation of Vajrabhairava*, compiled by Kyabje Phabongkha Rinpoche, translated by Sharpa Tulku with Richard Guard. Dharamsala: Library of Tibetan Works and Archives, 1991, p.11.

4   Mario I. Aguilar, Notes and Records I, June 2016.

5   I am aware that the transcriptions and ordering of materials presented in this chapter are of an ethnocentric nature and only correspond to my own notes, memories and interpretations. However, unlike other transcriptions of conversations and dialogue, this chapter is located within my own writings on dialogue and therefore they reflect my own emic understanding.

6   © Kabir Babu (Remembrance Sunday, 2013).

7   Emile Durkheim, 'Elementary Forms of Religious Life', in Michael Lambek (ed.) (2001) *A Reader in the Anthropology of Religion*. Oxford: Blackwell, p.38.

8   Roy Rappaport (1999) *Ritual and Religion in the Making of Humanity.* Cambridge: Cambridge University Press, pp.1–10.

9   Camaldoli as a hermitage for prayer was founded in 1023, and the Camaldolese Congregation was established under Pope Paschal II (1099–1118). He confirmed the congregation as an autonomous union of monasteries and hermitages under Camaldoli. See the ecclesiastical texts *Ad hoc nos* (1105) and *Gratias Deo* (1113) in the Vatican archives. For a fuller history of the Camaldolese see Peter-Damian Belisle (2002) 'Overview of Camaldolese History and Spirituality', in Peter-Damian Belisle (ed.) *The Privilege of Love: Camaldolese Benedictine Spirituality.* Collegeville, MN: Liturgical Press, pp.3–26.

10 Mario I. Aguilar (1988) *Being Oromo in Kenya.* Lawrenceville, NJ: Africa World Press.

11   Carlo Carretto (1910–1988) was a member of the Little Brothers of Jesus, the order inspired by the spirituality of Charles de Foucauld; see *Carlo Carretto: Essential Writings*, selected with an introduction by Robert Ellsberg. Maryknoll, NY: Orbis, 2007.

12   Thomas Matus and Robert Hale, 'The Camaldolese in Dialogue: Ecumenical and Interfaith Themes in the History of the Camaldolese Benedictines', in Belisle (ed.) *The Privilege of Love*, pp.157–68.

13   Bede Griffiths joined the Camaldolese Benedictines in 1980, when he was already the leader of the Saccinanda Ashram, Shantivanam, in Tamil Nadu; see Shirley Du Boulay (1998) *Beyond the Darkness: A Biography of Bede Griffiths*. London: Rider, pp.202–3. He had assumed the leadership of the ashram from Henri Le Saux (Swami Abhishiktananda).

14   For the background to these developments see Andy Marino (2015) *Narendra Modi: A Political Biography*. New York: HarperCollins, and Lance Prince (2016) *The Modi Effect: Inside Narendra Modi's Campaign to Transform India*. London: Hodder.

15   Shri Guru Granth Sahib, So Purakh, section 3, part 1.

16   © Sunra Babu. I am grateful to Sunra Babu for permission to reproduce her poem within this work.

17   Sunra Babu to Mario I. Aguilar, 6 July 2016.

18   Christopher Bartley (2015) *An Introduction to Indian Philosophy: Hindu and Buddhist Ideas from Original Sources*. London: Bloomsbury, p.3.

19   Balwant Singh Dhillon (2014) 'Formation of early Sikh identity', *Perspectives on Guru Granth Sahib IX*, 1–11.

20   Balwant Singh Dhillon (2014) *Haqiqat-i-Sikhan (An Eighteenth-Century Persian Source on the Origin and Rise of Sikh Religion)*. Amritsar: Guru Nanak Dev University. (Written in Punjabi.)

21   Hymns within the Granth are arranged in 31 ragas which were written in Persian, mediaeval Prakrit, Hindi, Marathi, old Panjabi, Multani, several local dialects as well as Arabic and Sanskrit.

CHAPTER 4

1   For an explanation of the seven different offices prayed by the monastic orders and the 1977 recommendations provided by the Sacred Congregation for the Sacraments and Divine Worship, see Anne M. Field OSB (ed.) (2001) *The Monastic Hours: Directory for the Celebration of the Work of God and Directive Norms for the Celebration of the Monastic Liturgy of the Hours*. Collegeville, MN: Liturgical Press.

2   The monastic office is different from the Roman breviary; see *The Monastic Diurnal: The Day Hours of the Monastic Breviary in Latin and English*. Farnborough: St. Michael's Abbey Press, 2011.

3   For an overview see Robert Taft SJ (1993) *The Liturgy of the Hours in East and West: The Origin of the Divine Office and Its Meaning for Today.* Collegeville, MN: Liturgical Press.

4   See Raimon Pannikar (2014) 'Letter to Abhishiktananda on Eastern and Western Monasticism', in *Mysticism and Spirituality: Spirituality – The Way of Life, Opera Omnia I.2.* Maryknoll, NY: Orbis, pp.253–77.

5   Panikkar, *Opera Omnia I.2*, p.255.

6   See 'Shantivanam's Daily Liturgy' in Mario I. Aguilar (2016) *Christian Ashrams, Hindu Caves and Sacred Rivers: Christian–Hindu Monastic Dialogue in India 1950–1993.* London and Philadelphia: Jessica Kingsley Publishers, pp.96–8.

7   However, Bede Griffiths went further than others who couldn't agree, for example, with the image of the Christ meditating in the lotus position resembling the Buddha; see Aguilar, *Christian Ashrams, Hindu Caves and Sacred Rivers*, p.96.

8   See for example John Paul II, Encyclical Letter *Ecclesia De Eucharistia*, 2003, where the first paragraph argues that 'the Church draws her life from the Eucharist'.

9   A survey in progress relating to the implementation of changes within the liturgy was published periodically. Thus in February 1966 a report from five continents, Asia, Australia, Africa, Latin America and North America, suggested that 'every Episcopal Conference in Asia has, quite significantly, urged Rome to allow them as much vernacular in the liturgy as possible', while problems of translation were highlighted, reporting that in the Philippines 66 languages were used and that the bishops had selected eight languages to be used for the liturgy; see 'Documentation Concilium. The Constitution on the Sacred Liturgy applied in Five Continents: A Survey of Progress', *Concilium*, *2/2*, February 1966, pp.66–82 at pp.66–7.

10 Sacred Congregation for Divine Worship, *Eucharistiae participationem* ('Circular Letter on the Eucharistic Prayers', 27 April 1973), §6. The full title is 'A circular letter to the Presidents of Episcopal Conferences: *Litterae Circulares ad conferentiarum praesides de precibus eucharisticis*'.

11 Dr John Wijngaards to Mario I. Aguilar, 3 February 2016. I am grateful to Dr Wijngaards for sending me a copy of the experimental text used during the 1970s in pastoral Indian settings and for pointing me to the theological work by Jacques Dupuis SJ.

12 Statement of the IV All India Liturgical Meeting, Bangalore, December 1973, §17, cited in J. Dupuis SJ (1974) 'The use of non-Christian Scriptures in Christian worship in India' (documentation), *Studia Missionalia 23*, 'Worship and Ritual', p.128.

13 For the full text of the 'Indian Rite' see Appendix 1.

14 Fr Dupuis SJ, who wrote the prayer, was investigated by the Vatican and some of his writings were deemed to be not in line with Catholic doctrine, and as a result for a few years he was not permitted to teach or write within Catholic universities and pastoral institutes.

15 See Paul M. Collins (2007) *Christian Inculturation in India*. London: Routledge; Michelle Voss Roberts (2014) *Tastes of the Divine: Hindu and Christian Theologies of Emotion*. New York: Fordham University Press; and Richard Fox Young (ed.) (2009) *India and the Indianness of Christianity: Essays on Understanding, Historical, Theological, and Biographical in Honor of Robert Eric Frykenberg*. Grand Rapids, MI: William B. Eerdmans.

16 'Saturday 21 July' (1984), in Thomas Matus (2009) *Ashram Diary: In India with Bede Griffiths*. Winchester and Washington: O Books, p.10.

17 Abhishiktananda to Sr Térèse de Jésus (Lemoine), 24 October 1966.

18 Morning prayers, Nalanda Hermitage, 20 July 2016.

19 Rig Veda 3.62.10.

20 See the possibilities of a universal spirituality in Wayne Teasdale (2001) *The Mystic Heart: Discovering a Universal Spirituality in the World's Religions*. Novato, CA: New World Library.

21 Office for the Liturgical Celebrations of the Supreme Pontiff, 'The Liturgy, Work of the Trinity/1: God the Father (Catechism of the Catholic Church [CCC 1077–1083])'.

22 Raimon Panikkar (2010) *The Rhythm of Being: The Unbroken Trinity, The Gifford Lectures, Edinburgh University*. Maryknoll, NY: Orbis, p.321.

23 Mundaka Upanishad Part I: Chapter 1.

24 Bodhicharyāvatāra 3.10.

25 Shatapatha Brahmana 2.2.4.1–8. Translation by Wendy Doniger (2015) *Hinduism: The Norton Anthology of World Religions*, ed. Jack Miles. New York: W.W. Norton, pp.94–5.

26 *Bede Griffiths: Essential Writings*, selected with an introduction by Thomas Matus. Maryknoll, NY: Orbis, 2004, p.121.

27 'Saturday 21 July' (1984), in Thomas Matus, *Ashram Diary*, p.10.

28 Fakir Lalon Shah, 'The Bird and the Cage, and the Flower', translation by David Haberman, in Doniger, *Hinduism*, pp.527–8.

29 Rig Veda 1.1.1.

30 Wendy Doniger, 'Humans, Animals, and Gods in the *Rig Veda* 1500–1000 BCE', *Hinduism*, pp.73–8 at p.75.

31 Mundaka Upanishad Part I: Chapter 1.

32 Holy See Press Office, 'Pope Francis appalled by the taking of hostages and the murder of a priest in a church near Rouen', 26 July 2016.

33 'France churches host Muslims for Mass', *BBC News*, 31 July 2016.

34 Panikkar, 'The Presence of God', in *Opera Omnia I.2*, pp.87–95 at p.92.

35 I note the recent contribution to this theme by Pierre-François de Béthune OSB (2016) *Welcoming Other Religions: A New Dimension of the Christian Faith*. Collegeville, MN: Liturgical Press.

36 Holy See Press Office, 'Prayer for peace and for an end to violence and terrorism in the Church of St. Francis', Poland, 31 July 2016, N. 160731a.

37 'Prayer for peace and for an end to violence and terrorism in the Church of St. Francis', Poland, 31 July 2016.

38 Raimon Panikkar, *Opera Omnia I.2*, p.313.

CHAPTER 5

1 Mandukya Upanishad, in Mario I. Aguilar (2016) *Christian Ashrams, Hindu Caves and Sacred Rivers: Christian–Hindu Monastic Dialogue in India 1950–1993*. London and Philadelphia: Jessica Kingsley Publishers, p.75.

2 Enzo Bianchi (2015) *Lectio Divina: From God's Word to Our Lives*. London: SPCK; Dom David Foster (2005) *Reading with God: Lectio Divina*. London: Continuum; Christine Valters Paintner (2012) *Lectio Divina: The Sacred Art*. London: SPCK.

3 Isa Upanishad.

4 Mario I. Aguilar (2011) *The Trappists of Tibhirine: Martyrs for a Christian–Muslim Dialogue (+1996)*. Santiago: Fundación Literaria Civilización.

5 Tenzin Gyatso, 14th Dalai Lama (2009) *For the Benefit of All Beings: A Commentary on the Way of the Bodhisattva*. Boston: Shambala.

6 Shantideva (2006) *The Way of the Bodhisattva: A Translation of the Bodhicharyāvatāra*. Boston: Shambhala; *The Upanishads*, translation from the Sanskrit with an introduction by Juan Mascaró. London: Penguin, 1965.

7 'Silence, the Pro-Logos and the Monk in Raimon Panikkar', in Aguilar, *Christian Ashrams, Hindu Caves and Sacred Rivers*, pp.143–58.

8 For some short descriptions of that period see Mario I. Aguilar (2010) *Amor y una máquina de escribir: La vida de Marcela Sepúlveda Troncoso 1955–1974 (Love and a Typewriter: The Life of Marcela Sepúlveda Troncoso 1955–1974)*. Santiago: Fundación Literaria Civilización; (2015) *Religion, Torture and the Liberation of God*. New York: Routledge.

9 It is an interesting fact that during 2016 a book on the Trinity has sold thousands of copies; see Richard Rohr with Mike Morrell (2016) *The Divine Dance: The Trinity and Your Transformation*. London: SPCK.

10 Mario I. Aguilar (1993) 'Dialogue with Waso Boorana traditional religious practices', *African Ecclesial Review 35*, 2, 101–14.

11 Shantideva also wrote a *Compendium for Training* (Shikshasamucchaya), which organizes the elements of a bodhisattva's practice.

12 Venerable Choje Lama Yeshe Losal Rimpoche to Mario I. Aguilar, St Andrews, 23 September 2016.

13 Gyilung Tashi Gyatso and Gyilung Thugchok Dorji (2009) *The Treasure of the Ancestral Clans of Tibet*, translated by Yeshi Dhondup. Dharamsala: Library of Tibetan Works and Archives.

14 See, for example, Tsong-Kha-Pa (2006) 'The Three Types of Persons', in *Lam Rim Chen Mo – The Great Treatise on the Stages of the Path to Enlightenment*. Ithaca, NY: Snow Lion Publications, pp.129–41.

15 Bodhicharyāvatāra III.12.

16 Tenzin Gyatso, *For the Benefit of All Beings*, p.3.

17 Bodhicharyāvatāra V.77.

18 Bodhicharyāvatāra III.8.

19 Bodhicharyāvatāra III.11.

20 Bodhicharyāvatāra X.55.

21 Parmananda R. Divarkar SJ (1988) 'Prólogo', in Anthony de Mello, *La oración de la rana*. Santander: Editorial Sal Terrae, pp.xiii–xv at p.xiv.

22 For a fuller essay on the issue of sources and the four *ashramas* or ways of life see 'Renunciation in the Upanishads 600–200 BCE', in Wendy Doniger (2015) *Hinduism: The Norton Anthology of World Religions*, ed. Jack Miles. New York: W.W. Norton, pp.105–6.

23 All through this chapter I use the English text: *The Upanishads*, translation from the Sanskrit with an introduction by Juan Mascaró. London: Penguin, 1965.

24 Ernesto Cardenal (2002) *Cosmic Canticle*. Willimantic, CT: Curbstone Press; Nicanor Parra (1986) *Poems and Antipoems*. New York: New Directions.

25 On Merton and Parra's correspondence, see Mario I. Aguilar (2011) *Thomas Merton: Contemplation and Political Action*. London: SPCK, pp.85–7.

26 Bede Griffiths (2003) *The Marriage of East and West*. Tucson, AZ: Medio Media, p.96.

27 Griffiths, *The Marriage of East and West*, p.92.

28 Raimon Panikkar (2014) *Mysticism and Spirituality: Mysticism, Fullness of Life, Opera Omnia I.1*. Maryknoll, NY: Orbis, p.218.

CHAPTER 6

1 Holy See Press Office, 'In Auschwitz-Birkenau: Francis visits in silence and writes in the Book of Honour, "Lord, forgiveness for so much cruelty"', 29 July 2016, N. 160729d.

2   Pope Francis visited Poland on the occasion of the XXXI World Youth Day, 27–31 July 2016.

3   John Paul II, 'Speech at Auschwitz', 7 June 1979.

4   Benedict XVI, 'Address: Visit to the Auschwitz Camp', Auschwitz-Birkenau, 28 May 2006.

5   Benedict XVI, 'Address: Visit to the Auschwitz Camp', Auschwitz-Birkenau, 28 May 2006.

6   Mario I. Aguilar (2015) *Religion, Torture and the Liberation of God.* New York: Routledge.

7   I note here the issue of suicide by several important survivors of the Shoah such as Benno Werzberger (Israel), Tadeusz Borowski (Poland), Paul Celan and Piotr Rawicz (France), Bruno Bettelheim (USA) and Primo Levi (Italy). The reflections by Elie Wiesel are quite pertinent to understand the extension of death by survivors and their despair at being isolated through their life witness; see Elie Wiesel (2000) 'Three Suicides', in *And the Sea is Never Full: Memoirs 1969–.* London: HarperCollins, pp.345–51.

8   For a fuller explanation of this silencing of the word see 'Silence, the Pro-Logos and the Monk in Raimon Panikkar', in Mario I. Aguilar (2016) *Christian Ashrams, Hindu Caves and Sacred Rivers: Christian–Hindu Monastic Dialogue in India 1950–1993.* London: Jessica Kingsley Publishers, pp.143–58.

9   Raimon Panikkar (2014) *Mysticism and Spirituality: Spirituality – The Way of Life, Opera Omnia I.2,* edited by M. Carrara Pavan. Maryknoll, NY: Orbis, p.122.

10 Panikkar, *Opera Omnia I.2,* p.122.

11 Panikkar, 'Sūtra 3: Silence over the Word', in *Opera Omnia I.2,* pp.163–6.

12 'Pope Francis visits Auschwitz-Birkenau museum and memorial', Vatican Radio, 29 July 2016.

13 'Memoria e silenzio: Durante la visita ad Auschwitz e Birkenau il Papa prega per le vittime della Shoah – L'invocazione al Signore e la richiesta di perdono per tanta crudeltà', *L'Osservatore Romano,* 30 July 2016.

14 The full two-hour video broadcast 'Pope Francis in Poland. Visit to the Auschwitz-Birkenau Concentration Camp', Vatican Television, is available at https://www.youtube.com/watch?v=FO6OCefhNn4, accessed on 2 December 2016.

15 According to the information provided by the Auschwitz-Birkenau Memorial and Museum, 'the first and oldest [part] was the so-called "main camp", later also known as "Auschwitz I" (the number of prisoners fluctuated around 15,000, sometimes rising above 20,000), which was established on the grounds and in the buildings of prewar Polish barracks.

The second part was the Birkenau camp (which held over 90,000 prisoners in 1944), also known as "Auschwitz II". This was the largest part of the Auschwitz complex. The Nazis began building it in 1941 on the site of the village of Brzezinka, three kilometers from Oswiecim. The Polish civilian population was evicted and their houses confiscated and demolished. The greater part of the apparatus of mass extermination was built in Birkenau and the majority of the victims were murdered here.' Available at http://auschwitz.org/en/history/kl-auschwitz-birkenau, accessed on 2 December 2016.

16 Damien Walne and Joan Flory (1983) *Totally Hers: St. Maximilian Kolbe.* High Wycombe, Bucks: Dites Publications.

17 Fabrice d'Almeida (2013) 'Prólogo', in Carl Schrade, *El veterano: Once años en los campos de concentración nazis.* Barcelona: Atico de los libros, pp.13–32 at p.23.

18 World Holocaust Remembrance Center, 'About the Righteous.' Available at www.yadvashem.org/righteous/about-the-righteous, accessed on 5 January 2017.

19 François Mitterrand and Elie Wiesel (1995) *Memoria a dos voces.* Buenos Aires: Editorial Andrés Bello, p.100.

20 See, for example, Alan Adelson (ed.) (1997) *The Diary of Dawid Sierakowiak.* London: Bloomsbury; Hélène Berr (2009) *Journal.* London: MacLehose Press; Samuel Drix (1995) *Witness: Surviving the Holocaust, Memoir.* London: Fount; Hella Pick (1996) *Simon Wiesenthal: A Life in Search of Justice.* Boston: Northeastern University Press; Olga Watkins with James Gillespie (2011) *A Greater Love.* Droxford, Hampshire: Splendid Books; Elie Wiesel (1997) *All Rivers Run to the Sea: Memoirs, Volume One 1928–1969.* London: HarperCollins.

21 Aguilar, *Religion, Torture and the Liberation of God.*

22 Mario I. Aguilar (2008) *A las puertas de la Villa Grimaldi: Poemas.* Santiago: Caliope Editores; (2009) *Retorno a la Villa Grimaldi.* Santiago: Caliope Ediciones; (2010) *The Historiography of the Chilean Commission on Prison and Torture 2003–2009.* Santiago: Fundación Literaria Civilización; (2010) *The Historiography of the Patio 29: General Cemetery, Santiago, Chile 1973–2009.* Santiago: Fundación Literaria Civilización; (2010) *Identification of Human Remains (N.N.) at Patio 29, General Cemetery, Santiago, Chile, December 2009.* Santiago: Fundación Literaria Civilización; (2010) *Burials and Memory of the GAP in Chile during September 2010: Historiography in Chile's Bicentenary.* Santiago: Fundación Literaria Civilización; (2010) *Amor y revolución en la vida de Muriel Dockendorff 1951–1974/Love and Revolution in the Life of Muriel Dockendorff 1951–1974.* Santiago: Fundación Literaria Civilización; (2010) *Amor y una máquina de escribir: La vida de Marcela Sepúlveda*

Troncoso 1955–1974/Love and a Typewriter: The Life of Marcela Sepúlveda Troncoso 1955–1974. Santiago: Fundación Literaria Civilización; (2010) *The Theology of Marcella Althaus-Reid: Indecent Theology and Queer Narratives.* Santiago: Fundación Literaria Civilización; (2010) *The Ovens of Lonquén: Historiography, Memory and Human Rights in Chile 1973–2010.* Santiago: Fundación Literaria Civilización; (2011) *Identification of Human Remains (N.N.) at Chihuío (Panguipulli), Chile, July 2011.* Santiago: Fundación Literaria Civilización; (2011) *Identification of Human Remains (N.N.) at Patio 29, General Cemetery, Santiago, Chile, March 2011.* Santiago: Fundación Literaria Civilización.

23 Wiesel, *And the Sea is Never Full*, p.82.

24 Mark Tatz (1997) 'Introduction', *Candragomin's Twenty Verses on the Bodhisattva Vow and Its Commentary by Sakya Dragpa Gyaltsen.* Dharamsala: Library of Tibetan Works and Archives, pp.xiii–xiv.

25 Kena Upanishad Part II.

26 Katha Upanishad Part I.

27 Katha Upanishad Part I.

28 © Ramesh Babu, 21 April 2014, 8.44pm, Bathinda (translated by Kabir Babu).

29 Mitterrand and Wiesel, *Memoria a dos voces*, p.69.

30 'The Nobel Peace Prize Acceptance Speech Delivered by Elie Wiesel in Oslo on 10 December, 1986', in Elie Wiesel (2006) *Night.* London: Penguin, pp.117–20 at p.118.

31 'The Nobel Peace Prize Acceptance Speech Delivered by Elie Wiesel in Oslo on 10 December, 1986', p.120.

32 Pope Francis, *Laudato si', Carta Encíclica de S.S. Francisco: Sobre el cuidado de la casa común.* Rome, 24 May 2015. Santiago: Conferencia Episcopal de Chile.

33 *Laudato si'* §2.

34 *Laudato si'* §3, cf. John XXIII, *Pacem in terris* (1963).

35 *Laudato si'* §4, cf. Paul VI, *Octogesima adveniens* (14 May 1971), 21, and 'Discurso a la FAO en su 25 aniversario', 16 November 1970, AAS 62, p.833.

36 *Laudato si'* §5, cf. John Paul II, *Redemptor hominis* (4 March 1979) §15, *Catquesis* (17 January 2001) §4 and *Centesimus annus* (1 May 1991) §38.

37 *Laudato si'* §6, cf. Benedict XVI, 'Discurso al Deutscher Bundestag, Berlín', 22 September 2011, AAS 103, p.664.

38 *Laudato si'* §§7–9.

39 *Laudato si'* §8. Ecumenical Patriarch Bartholomew, 'Speech in Santa Barbara, California', 8 November 1997; see John Chryssavgis (2012) *On Earth as in Heaven: Ecological Vision and Initiatives of Ecumenical Patriarch Bartholomew.* New York: Fordham University Press.

40 *Laudato si'* §9 and Ecumenical Patriarch Bartholomew, 'Global Responsibility and Ecological Sustainability: Closing Remarks', I Vértice de Halki, Istanbul, 20 June 2012.

41 *Laudato si'* §201.

42 'Ant', in Vinay Dharwadker (2005) *Kabir: The Weaver's Songs.* New Delhi: Penguin India, pp.119–20, cited in Sunder John Boopalan (2016) 'Hybridity's Ambiguity (Gift or Threat?): Marginality as Rudder', in Peniel Jesudason Rufus Rajkumar and Joseph Prabhakar Dayam (eds) *Many Yet One? Multiple Religious Belonging.* Geneva: World Council of Churches Publications, pp.135–48 at p.135.

APPENDIX 1

1 This Eucharistic Prayer was used and prayed by Catholic priests in India throughout the 1970s. Following Vatican II's directives on the use of vernacular languages and liturgical forms for the celebration of the Eucharist, experimental texts for the celebration of the Eucharist, including Eucharistic Prayers and local rites, were developed in Asia, Africa and Latin America after the end of the Council. I am grateful to Dr John Wijngaards for sending me a copy of the text I reproduce, which was the pastoral text for the 'Indian Eucharistic Prayer' used in many parishes and Catholic communities in India.

APPENDIX 2

1 Morning prayers, Nalanda Hermitage, 20 July 2016.

APPENDIX 3

1 Evening/Night Prayers of Arunachala Hermitage, © Mario I. Aguilar.

2 The gats are the steps where pilgrims go into the water in Varanasi.

3 © Mario I. Aguilar, Arunachala Hermitage, 14 May 2016.

APPENDIX 4

1 'Saturday 21 July' (1984), in Thomas Matus (2009) *Ashram Diary: In India with Bede Griffiths.* Winchester and Washington: O Books, p.10.

2 Fakir Lalon Shah, 'The Bird and the Cage, and the Flower', translation by David Haberman, in Wendy Doniger (2015) *Hinduism: The Norton Anthology of World Religions*, ed. Jack Miles. New York: W.W. Norton, pp.527–8.

3 For the full text of the 'Indian Rite' see Appendix 1.

APPENDIX 5

1   Mundaka Upanishad Part I: Chapter 1.
2   Bodhicharyāvatāra 3.10.
3   Shatapatha Brahmana 2.2.4.1–8, translation by Wendy Doniger (2015) *Hinduism: The Norton Anthology of World Religions*, ed. Jack Miles. New York: W.W. Norton, pp.94–5.
4   For the full text of the 'Indian Rite' see Appendix 1.

APPENDIX 6

1   Year of Interfaith Dialogue, University of St Andrews. Available at www.yearofinterfaithdialogue.com, accessed on 2 December 2016.
2   © Mario I. Aguilar, July 2016.
3   © Mario I. Aguilar. Written in Amritsar, June 2016.

INDEX

Mario I. Aguilar is Professor of Religion & Politics and Director of the Centre for the Study of Religion & Politics at the University of St Andrews. He is also a poet and an eremitic Camaldolese Benedictine Oblate, and has published widely in his interests in the theology of contemplation, the history of religion and issues of interfaith dialogue.